15
minute vegan
on a budget

*fast, modern vegan food
that costs less*

Katy Beskow

photography by Dan Jones

quadrille

contents

introduction

I'm often asked whether living a vegan lifestyle is expensive – there are a lot of misconceptions of vegans eating unpronounceable grains and an excess of avocados, shopping in exclusive food stores, and having high energy bills due to boiling all those pulses. But the honest, surprising-to-some answer is: no.

My own journey into veganism has humble beginnings, when I moved to London as a student back in 2006. With just enough money to cover rent and bills, I started shopping at a local fruit and vegetable market to make savings. The market was intoxicating, with vibrant and exotic produce, as well as cheap and fast-cooking rice, canned beans, and lentils. Buying seasonal, vegan produce gave me a way to get creative in the kitchen, as well as inspiring what would become an unexpected career in food writing.

You don't need specialist ingredients to cook great vegan meals. Everything you need is available at the supermarket – from fresh vegetables and a variety of non-dairy milks, to an array of herbs and, of course, a selection of beans and pulses. This is great for those of us on a budget, as this includes supermarket-own brands delivering great quality at affordable prices. There's no need to even step foot into a pricey health-food shop (and your wallet will be relieved to see that there's no avocado, quinoa, or tofu in sight!).

Just like any diet, one high in processed foods will be expensive. There is now a good, widely available selection of vegan ready meals, pizzas, and snacks, which is convenient, and a sign that the demand for vegan food is increasing. However, these items can be costly. Avoid these expensive vegan meals, and buy the basic ingredients you need to cook great food at home at a fraction of the price.

You'll be pleased to learn that vegan cooking is fast, as the ingredients are easy to prepare and transform into something hearty, nutritious, and delicious. Being short of time and on a budget doesn't mean you have to sacrifice great food. You'll find all the recipes in this book are full of flavour, creativity and, of course, are as effortless and quick as possible. There are also fewer food safety risks compared to storing, preparing, and cooking meat, fish, eggs, and dairy; just ensure you store non-dairy milk in the refrigerator and cook beans and pulses thoroughly.

People are choosing a vegan lifestyle for various reasons, including animal ethics, sustainability, health improvement, and wanting to understand where their food is really from and how it's processed. It is also now common for people to choose a vegan diet to save money. Plant proteins are remarkably cheaper than meat, fish, or dairy products. Need convincing? Price up my Lentil ragu (page 123) compared to a ragu made with beef mince. It's easier and quicker to cook, lower in fat, and costs much less to put together. If you feel daunted by the idea of vegan cooking, let these recipes show you how easy it really is – from shopping to preparation.

Whatever your reasons for starting a vegan lifestyle, or adding more vegan meals into your diet, and regardless of how much money you are able, or want, to spend on food, it's important to remember that veganism is accessible to all. Have fun with cooking, enjoy your time in the kitchen, and create delicious, vegan meals in moments.

10 tips for smart shopping on a budget

Cooking delicious, fast, vegan food starts with having the right ingredients. Shopping on a budget doesn't have to be difficult; it just requires some preparation, knowing where to shop, and how to find the best quality ingredients for the lowest prices.

1) When meal planning, consider breakfast, lunch, dinner, and snacks so you can stock up on the ingredients you need for trying new recipes, or creating your family favourites. It's also worth noting how many portions the recipe makes; if you make more than needed, don't forget to freeze the left overs and you have a homemade ready meal available for another week's meal plan. The short investment of time it takes to create a weekly meal plan can really make financial savings. Think of a meal plan as a list of what you're going to cook and eat for the week – it's simple and effective.

2) Before writing a shopping list, take a look inside your fridge, freezer, and cupboards. Note what you already have and think about how to use it while creating a meal plan for the week. For example, you may already have half a bag of onions from the week before, along with frozen peas and rice in the cupboard, so you've already got the basic ingredients for Kedgeree with paprika yoghurt (page 129). This reduces waste and the cost of your food-shop bill.

3) Write a shopping list and stick to it! After creating your meal plan, you know exactly what you're going to cook and eat, with ingredients you already have available

and what else you need to purchase. Mindfully purchase exactly what you need, and try not to go shopping on an empty stomach – you'll only be tempted into pricey extras that you haven't budgeted for.

4) Choose where is best to shop. Whether you prefer a large supermarket for its wide selection of products, a small supermarket due to close proximity, or online shopping for convenience, you'll find vegan items readily available. While larger, well-known supermarkets may stock more choice of specialist vegan products such as non-dairy cheeses, plant-based milks, and vegan chocolates, budget chain supermarkets are certainly catching up with their selection. Veganism is growing, and the availability of products is a reflection of this.

5) Consider shopping at fruit and vegetable markets for good prices on seasonal produce. Markets are often useful when buying products in bulk if you are batch-cooking or preparing meals for a family. Generally, the overheads of the market traders are less than supermarket chains, so savings can be passed onto the consumer. It's great to support local traders too.

6) When you're refilling the spice rack, take a look at the range and price of spices at Indian, Middle Eastern, Asian, and Chinese shops and supermarkets. You'll be able to purchase more for your money! While you're there, check out the rice, egg-free noodles, and coconut milk, as these items are often cheaper too.

7) When shopping in a large supermarket, look in the world-food aisle for store-cupboard essentials such as chickpeas, green lentils, coconut milk, tahini, soy sauce, rice, and egg-free noodles. These staple ingredients are often remarkably cheaper in this aisle.

8) One certain way to reduce your food bill is to switch your branded products for supermarket-own brand products. Supermarket "value" ranges are another great switch, particularly for dried pasta and spaghetti, as these basic items are less likely to contain eggs in order to keep costs low (always check the ingredients). Challenge yourself and your family to determine if you can tell the difference between branded products and own-brand products. Your wallet will thank you!

9) Reduced price, use-by date, "yellow sticker" items may seem like a bargain, but don't be tempted into buying something you won't eat just because it has been reduced to sell. If you make a purchase, eat or cook with it by the next day, or freeze it for use in the future (but don't forget it's in the freezer!). Similarly, be cautious of coupons and vouchers, and purchase only what you will actually use, no matter the discount.

10) Pre-prepared food isn't always bad, especially when cooking on a budget. For example, cooked beetroot that has been vacuum-packed is convenient and saves you a long cooking time at home. Chopped and frozen butternut squash, sweet potato, seasonal fruit, and herbs are great buys to reduce preparation and cooking time, then you can use as much as you need before returning the rest to the freezer, resulting in no food waste.

what to buy

Cook up fast, delicious, and cost-effective vegan meals with the addition of a few staples to your store cupboard, refrigerator, and freezer.

vegetables

Vegetables are the basis of a balanced vegan meal, so instead of thinking of vegetables as a side dish, make them the star of the show! Familiarize yourself with what vegetables are in season (there are multiple online resources) as you'll find them cheaper in shops and markets when there's an abundance, and they'll taste better too. Consider buying "versatile vegetables", which can be used in varying ways – for example, spinach can be used in a curry or as a salad leaf, and broccoli can be stir-fried, quick-roasted, or served as a crudité. Think about how you can finish the pack and write this into your weekly meal plan to avoid waste and save you money.

Prepared vegetables may set you back more money than their whole counterparts, so consider if it's worth it for the sake of a few moments' chopping. Some pre-prepared vegetables, such as vacuum-packed cooked beetroot, save hours of roasting time and can be used instantly in a recipe and don't cost remarkably more, so weigh up what works out as money-saving, time-saving, and energy-saving for you. Frozen vegetables are a convenient way to use vegetables in your cooking for a low price with less waste, as you'll just use what you need and return the remainder to the freezer.

Peas, sweet potato, butternut squash, peppers, and sweetcorn retain their flavour and texture when frozen, and are an economical and convenient addition to your kitchen. Some supermarkets and greengrocers offer excellent value "wonky vegetable" boxes, which contain non-standard shapes of popular vegetables – who cares what shape the vegetables are when they are getting chopped up into a recipe? These boxes are especially good for families, or if you are batch-cooking. If you're cooking for one, buy loose, unpackaged vegetables to give you the amount you need for a lower cost.

fruits

Not only do various fruits make an excellent addition to puddings, savoury dishes, and salads, think about swapping your mid-morning or afternoon snack for a piece of fruit – you'll find it's a good saving compared to snacking on crisps or chocolate (and better for your health). Similarly to vegetables, enjoy fresh fruits seasonally for their best flavour and lowest price. Eating seasonally also enables you to try new fruits that perhaps are outside of what you would normally purchase. Soft fruits such as berries and bananas, are versatile as a snack, to throw into a smoothie, or use in a pudding, and they will cook in next to no time.

Canned fruits allow you to enjoy fruit that may be out of season, store it for longer than fresh, and has the benefit of low or no cooking time. Need convincing? Try my Pear and chocolate crumble (page 140). Frozen fruits are again excellent for enjoying fruits out of season, particularly when they will be cooked into a dessert or blended into a smoothie. Although you may not buy lemons and limes as an essential, they add an instant burst of flavour to any dish, with very little effort. Always choose unwaxed lemons and limes, as these fruits particularly can be coated with shellac, which is an animal ingredient, used to make the fruit appear shiny. For cheaper fruit, consider signing up to an allotment-share programme, or look into "pick your own" days at local farms.

non-dairy milk, yoghurt, cheese, and butter

There is now a wide range of non-dairy milks available at supermarkets, including soya, oat, almond, cashew, coconut, and rice milks. A few years ago, these were expensive to buy, but now the market has grown and prices are coming down. For the most cost-effective non-dairy milks, opt for a supermarket-own brand, and choose one that has been ultra-heat treated (UHT), meaning it does not need to be stored in a refrigerator until opened and has a long shelf life. It is worth trying a few non-dairy milks to find your favourite. I find the most versatile is unsweetened soya milk, as it can be used in hot drinks, as well as savoury and sweet cooking.

Dairy-free yoghurts can vary in price, often due to the added flavours, so buy a large pot of unsweetened soya yoghurt and simply add the flavour yourself, whether it is lemon or frozen fruits, or use the yoghurt as a cooling dip for a savoury dish. Most large supermarkets now stock a range of soft and hard vegan cheeses. The best value vegan cheeses are often the supermarket-own brands, but shop around to find one you love. Vegan margarine (butter) is readily available in supermarkets. There's no need to spend a small fortune in health-food shops for any of these non-dairy items as they are widely available in supermarkets.

herbs and spices

Having a selection of herbs, spices, and spice blends available in the kitchen means you can create exciting and delicious dishes using basic store-cupboard ingredients. Woody herbs such as rosemary, thyme, sage, and oregano can give the flavour of a dish being slow-cooked for hours, when it's actually been cooked in just 15 minutes. These herbs are preserved well in dried form and are available at supermarkets in convenient jars. Leafy herbs such as flat-leaf parsley, coriander, basil, and mint may not be considered an essential on your shopping list when on a budget, but they lift a recipe with layers of freshness and flavour. These herbs are best used in fresh leaf form and can be kept fresher for longer when stored stem-down in a glass of water in a cool place. You could also consider growing herbs from a window box or small patch in the garden.

A few basic ground spices, such as cinnamon, ginger, and turmeric, can be versatile in both sweet and savoury dishes. You may find these spices cheaper when bought in bulk or from Asian supermarkets. Store fresh ginger root in the freezer and grate from frozen into stir-fries and curries. Spice blends such as chilli powder, garam masala, Chinese five spice, and jerk seasoning offer hits of flavour with very little preparation on your behalf, as the spices have been expertly blended. Add dried herbs and spices to your collection as you need them, and don't forget that they are a great gift to give and receive! Keep a small jar of curry paste in the fridge, ready to pack a flavour punch when you have little time to cook.

beans and pulses

Beans and pulses are a major source of protein in the vegan diet, and they just happen to be cheap, healthy, and delicious too. Canned beans and pulses are cheap and widely available, and also remove the long soaking and cooking time that they require when dried. Simply open the can, drain away the liquid, then thoroughly rinse them under cold running water to remove any "canned" taste. Bulk buying of dried beans and pulses may be cheaper, but consider the gas or electric energy required to cook them. If this is a better option for you, consider batch-cooking the beans or pulses, then cool and freeze them in 400g (14oz) quantities, ready for quick recipes in the future. Have a selection of beans and pulses available such as chickpeas, red kidney beans, butterbeans, and green lentils.

nuts and seeds

Nuts and seeds add instant texture, flavour, and crunch to any dish, as well as being nutritious powerhouses of energy! Prices can vary, but they are cheaper when bought in a big pack in supermarkets. Broken, flaked, and non-standard shapes can be found cheaper, and they last for ages in the cupboard. Hazelnuts and sesame seeds are versatile for snacking and to use in recipes.

pasta

Most dried pasta bought in supermarkets is egg-free and vegan friendly, but always check the ingredients before buying. Pasta is cheap, fast to cook, and easy to store in a cupboard, as well as being the basis for many lunches and dinners. If you have no preference about the shape of pasta, check out a supermarket's basic low-cost variety, as you can purchase a pack for a low cost, including penne or fusilli, depending on the store.

rice

Not only is it delicious and full of energy, rice is an affordable ingredient to create a side dish, pilaf, or pudding. Basmati, flaked, jasmine, and American long grain have the shortest cooking times, whereas brown and wild rice need longer to cook. Tonnes of cooked rice is wasted every year; this can be down to overestimating volumes of uncooked rice – a good rule of thumb is to consider that the volume will double when cooked, and 80–90g (2¾–3¼oz) of uncooked rice will serve one person.

Often, people are afraid to eat leftover rice due to a bacterium that can develop, however, this risk is reduced if the rice is chilled quickly and refrigerated until used. It's safe to eat leftover rice that has been kept refrigerated within 24 hours, just ensure it is thoroughly reheated before eating.

oil

With a large selection of oils available, it can be hard to know which to buy and use for your cooking. Choose a mild-flavoured and cost-effective oil, such as sunflower or olive oil, for general cooking, and choose an extra virgin olive or cold-pressed rapeseed oil only for drizzling over finished dishes, when you want the peppery flavour of a more expensive oil. One general cooking oil, such as sunflower oil, and one oil for dressing, such as extra virgin olive oil, is sufficient for cooking on a budget.

salt

Salt is a natural flavour enhancer that, when used in moderation, lifts the taste of any dish. Opt for good-quality sea-salt flakes that can be crushed gently between your fingers.

sugar

Enjoy the natural sweetness of sugar in puddings, and use it to take away the acidity of tomatoes in savoury dishes, but consume in moderation. Most of the sugar sold in the UK is vegan friendly as it is not combined with, or filtered through, animal products. Contact the supplier if you are unsure of the status of a brand.

canned chopped tomatoes and passata

Chopped tomatoes and smooth passata are the basis for so many recipes, including casseroles, curries, and pasta sauces. These items are cheap and have a long shelf life, as well as being easy to throw into a pan to create a hearty meal. Switch to a supermarket basic brand and see if you can tell the difference in taste.

canned coconut milk

Where coconut milk is used in this book, it refers to the canned variety. It is thick, luxurious, and silky when added to a soup, spiced dish, or dessert. Find the lowest-cost cans of coconut milk in the world-food aisle of supermarkets, or in Asian supermarkets. Full-fat varieties have the best flavour.

vegetable stock

Ensure vegetable stock cubes or bouillon are vegan, as they can often contain milk as a bulking agent. Use to add instant seasoning to soups and casseroles, or make your own by simmering peelings of vegetables and stalks of fresh herbs in water, then freezing into tubs for when you need to use it.

Kitchen essentials

You don't need a large kitchen with an extensive array of gadgets in order to make fantastic, home-cooked meals. Add to your equipment collection over time, or as you can afford to do so.

A few good-quality knives will make food preparation much easier. Buy the best you can afford – you'll only need a small, medium, large, and bread knife. Look for knives that are weighty, as these will reduce the effort needed when chopping. Look after your knives by chopping onto a wooden chopping board to absorb the impact. A food processor can chop vegetables in a matter of seconds, which is convenient and effortless, but can be a costly appliance to purchase.

Whip up silken soups, quick breadcrumbs, and smooth houmous with a jug blender. For best results, choose a blender with over 1000W capabilities. A high-powered jug blender is an investment piece, but may be unaffordable or take up too much space in a small kitchen. Hand blenders are a good alternative, but may need a longer blending time and a little more effort.

One appliance that will save you money on food in the long run is a freezer. Use it to store frozen food essentials, including vegetables and fruits, as well as batch-cooked meals stored in airtight, labelled containers. Keep root ginger fresher for longer by storing it in the freezer and using it from frozen by grating it into your cooking. Can't think of a way to use up those fresh herbs? Chop the herbs and freeze them in ice-cube trays with water, then simply pop them into your next curry or casserole.

To cook in 15 minutes or less, choose pans that are silver or black inside, as they heat up quickly. You'll need a small, medium, and large saucepan; a griddle pan; and a wok for its concave shape that quickly transfers heat to the food. Baking trays can be purchased cheaply in home-wear shops and large supermarkets. Casserole dishes that are lined with a white inner are best saved for slow-cooked meals.

Make the most of your microwave by using it for more than just reheating. Cook basmati rice in just 10 minutes, steam fresh vegetables, or bake my Peanut butter melt-in-the-middle chocolate pudding (page 150). A microwave of 850W will heat your food evenly and quickly.

A Y-peeler is a quick and efficient way to peel vegetables. Y-peelers are simple and comfortable to use, as well as taking off just the right amount of vegetable peel, leaving you with more vegetable to eat. Pick one up for under £5 to make your preparation effortless.

Reduce food waste in seven easy ways (and keep more money in your pocket!)

1) Store your ingredients in the correct place to extend their shelf life and preserve quality. Keep root vegetables and onions in a cool, dark place. Store leafy green vegetables, apples, and grapes in the fridge between 1–4°C (34–39°F). Bread will become dry if stored in the fridge, however, if you plan on using it just for toast, it will certainly extend its life. Opened jars are best kept in a cool, dry place.

2) Before you start cooking, consider the quantity of ingredients you really need to use. An average portion size for uncooked rice is between 80–90g (2¾–3¼oz) per person, and allow 80–100g (2¾–3½oz) dried pasta per person. Cooking a larger quantity than needed of these basic ingredients can be costly and wasteful. If you intentionally cook more than needed so you can save some for another time, make sure you plan when you are going to use it up – and stick to it!

3) Treat use-by dates on food labelling as guidelines and not rules. Imagine that your food doesn't have packaging or a use-by date. Use your senses to determine if it is edible and, of course, use your common sense. If a vegetable appears a little limp, it can be chopped up and used in a cooked dish, but if there is visible mould or an odour, it shouldn't be eaten in the interests of food safety.

4) Have a selection of stackable food storage boxes and labels to hand for storing leftovers. This will maximize the space in your freezer and allow you to recognize what is in each box (it's harder than you might think when a meal is frozen!). Keep leftovers of sauces in clean glass jars in the fridge, again to make them easy to recognize and locate, and to keep them fresher for longer.

5) Rotate the items in your fridge, freezer, and cupboards to ensure that everything gets used before it passes its best quality and taste. This also reminds you of what you have available before you go shopping, so you can create meals around these products.

6) Make an informal list of the food you throw away, so you can recognize any patterns. Throwing away half a loaf of bread? Think about how better to store it and use it up. Throwing away that leftover pasta sauce you made last week? Remember to add leftovers to your meal plan. Throwing away an unopened bag of spinach? Base your shopping list around what you're actually going to cook that week.

7) Get creative with your leftover ingredients and cooked foods! Reducing waste and saving money on food bills doesn't have to be a struggle – there is a world of new recipes and meals available when you think outside of the box. Have fun with it!

LOVE YOUR LEFTOVERS

salt and vinegar potato peel crisps

Instead of mindlessly throwing away those potato peelings, use them to bake these moreish crisps. I love salt-and-vinegar-flavoured snacks, but you can mix it up by adding smoked paprika, chilli powder, or garam masala. Load into a bowl and enjoy, or store in an airtight container for up to three days. Bake these using the discarded potato peels from the Cajun-spiced potatoes (page 100) recipe.

Serves 2

Peelings of 4 thoroughly washed large potatoes

3 tbsp sunflower oil

Sprinkle of malt vinegar

Generous pinch of fine sea salt

Thinner peelings result in crisper snacks, so use a vegetable peeler for the crunchiest crisps. Thicker peelings may need a longer cooking time.

Preheat the oven to 200°C/Gas mark 6.

Arrange the potato peelings on a baking tray and drizzle over the oil. Use your hands to rub the oil over all surfaces of the peelings.

Sprinkle with malt vinegar, then bake for 10 minutes until golden and crisp.

Remove from the oven and season with sea salt.

lemon linguine with crispy broad beans

Lemons store well in the fridge, but if you're struggling to find a way to use them up, try this simple pasta. Broad beans are great to have in the freezer, as the freezing process barely changes the texture of the beans, and it means you can enjoy the taste of summer without the out-of-season cost. You can also find excellent olive oil at low cost supermarkets. As it is more expensive than other cooking oils, use for drizzling on pasta and salads as a little taste of luxury.

Serves 2

1 tbsp sunflower oil

4 tbsp frozen broad beans

140g (5oz) dried linguine (ensure egg free)

Zest and juice of 2 unwaxed lemons

Generous drizzle of extra virgin olive oil

Generous pinch of sea salt flakes

Small handful of chives, finely chopped

Bring the lemons to room temperature before making this dish and you'll get more juice out of the fruit.

Heat the sunflower oil in a frying pan over a medium–high heat and cook the broad beans for 7–8 minutes until they begin to crisp up.

In the meantime, add the linguine to a large saucepan of boiling water and simmer for 8–10 minutes until al dente, then drain.

Stir the lemon zest and juice through the linguine and return to the heat for 1 minute, then drizzle over the olive oil and season with sea salt.

Stir through the crispy broad beans and scatter with the chives. Serve immediately.

red onion relish

Transform neglected red onions into this sweet and tangy relish. Perfect served with Pantry antipasti salad (page 69).

Makes 1 small pot

---

2 tbsp sunflower oil

4 large red onions, peeled and finely sliced

1 tsp dried thyme

2 tsp soft brown sugar

2 tsp balsamic vinegar

Pinch of sea salt

Allow the relish to cool fully, then spoon into a clean jar. Keep refrigerated for up to two weeks.

Suitable for freezing.

Heat the oil in a large saucepan over a medium–high heat and cook the onions for 5 minutes, stirring frequently.

Stir in the thyme and sugar and reduce to a medium heat. Cook for a further 8 minutes, stirring to avoid sticking.

Remove from the heat and stir through the balsamic vinegar. Season with sea salt.

Serve as a hot or cold condiment.

pitta chips

Don't throw away those stale pitta breads lurking in the packet! Bake them into crunchy little chips – perfect for dipping into Butter bean houmous (page 68).

Serves 2

2 pitta breads, halved lengthways, each half sliced into small triangles

1 tbsp sunflower oil

Pinch of ground cumin

Pinch of dried coriander leaf

Pinch of sea salt

Pitta chips are an expensive shop-bought snack, but are cheap and easy to make with store-cupboard ingredients. Store in an airtight container for up to three days.

Preheat the oven to 180°C/Gas mark 4.

Place the pitta triangles on a baking tray, then brush them on both sides with the oil using a pastry brush.

Sprinkle over the ground cumin and dried coriander and bake for 8–10 minutes until golden and crisp.

Remove from the oven and season with sea salt.

bubble and squeak

Save that leftover mash and make the ultimate British comfort food – bubble and squeak. You can add any extra vegetables you have to this, but this is my favourite combination for a beautiful winter warmer. Serve with lashings of onion gravy; or for a fresher alternative, spoon over a little Italian salsa verde (page 24).

Serves 2

3 tbsp sunflower oil

1 onion, peeled and finely chopped

4 leaves of cavolo nero, stems removed and roughly chopped

1 carrot, peeled and grated

2 tbsp frozen peas

6 rounded tbsp leftover mashed potatoes (prepared with non-dairy milk and vegan butter)

Cavolo nero, dark green cabbage, or kale all work well in this recipe.

Heat 1 tablespoon of the oil in a frying pan over a high heat and cook the onion, cavolo nero, carrot, and peas for 2 minutes until the onion begins to soften.

Carefully spoon the hot vegetables into a bowl with the leftover mashed potatoes and stir to combine.

Heat another 1 tablespoon of oil in the same frying pan, then spoon in the mashed potato mixture, press down, and smooth it flat. Cook over a high heat for 5–6 minutes until a golden crust has formed.

Remove from the heat and place a plate over the pan. Carefully flip the semi-cooked bubble and squeak onto the plate, put the pan back onto the heat with the remaining tablespoon of oil, and return the bubble and squeak to the pan to cook the other side for 5 minutes until golden.

Turn out onto a plate and serve hot, sharing out as desired.

carrot and onion bhajis

My favourite Indian snacks are onion bhajis – not the type that come from a packet in the supermarket, but the aromatic, straight-out-of-hot-oil kind. I love using up unloved carrots in this recipe, even those slightly limp ones that live at the back of the vegetable drawer.

Makes about 8

1 medium carrot, peeled and grated

1 onion, peeled and finely sliced

1 tsp cumin seeds

1 tsp garam masala

½ tsp mild chilli powder

1 tsp fine sea salt

5 tbsp plain flour

500ml (17½fl oz/2 cups) sunflower oil, for frying

Juice of ½ unwaxed lemon

Cook 3–4 bhajis at a time to ensure they don't stick to each other in the pan.

Combine the carrot and onion in a bowl, then stir through the cumin seeds, garam masala, chilli powder, salt and flour.

Mix in 50ml (1¾fl oz/scant ¼ cup) of cold water to form a thick batter.

Heat the oil in a deep saucepan until hot (test this by dropping a small amount of batter into the oil; it should rise and become golden), then carefully spoon tablespoon-sized portions of batter into the oil. Cook for 4–5 minutes until golden, then carefully remove with a slotted spoon and drain on kitchen paper.

Squeeze over the lemon juice and serve hot with sauces of your choice.

italian salsa verde

Brighten up any casserole, soup, or roasted vegetables with this zingy sauce. Use up leftover leafy herbs from the garden, window box or fridge, and prepare the traditional way, using a knife to chop instead of a food processor. Delicious served with Bubble and squeak (page 21).

Makes 1 small pot

30g (1oz) flat-leaf parsley (leaves and stalks), finely chopped

Generous handful of basil, finely chopped

Generous handful of mint, finely chopped

1 clove of garlic, peeled and finely grated

1 tsp Dijon mustard

Juice of ½ unwaxed lemon

4 tbsp extra virgin olive oil

Leafy herbs work better than woody herbs in this sauce, so keep any rosemary, sage, and thyme for another recipe.

Suitable for freezing.

Combine the parsley, basil, mint, and garlic in a bowl.

Stir in the mustard and squeeze in the lemon juice. Mix in the oil until combined.

Allow to stand for at least 10 minutes to allow the flavours to develop.

five-spice fried rice

Cooked too much rice? Don't let it go to waste! This full-of-flavour fried rice is ready in under 8 minutes and is the perfect accompaniment to Stir-fried beetroot, ginger and lemon (page 105). If you've never cooked with leftover rice before, check out my tips on pages 10–11.

Serves 2 as a side dish

1 tbsp sunflower oil

4 spring onions, finely chopped

4 radishes, finely sliced

1 carrot, peeled and finely sliced

2 tbsp podded fresh or frozen edamame beans

1 red chilli, deseeded and finely sliced

1 clove of garlic, peeled and finely sliced

1 tsp Chinese five spice powder

8 tbsp leftover cooked basmati rice

1 tbsp dark soy sauce

Small handful of coriander, roughly torn

Chinese five spice is a blend of five classic spices (cinnamon, star anise, fennel, cloves, and ginger) that adds Eastern flavours to a dish, with little effort on your part as it comes pre-mixed in jars. Take a look at the supermarket spice aisle, or in a Chinese supermarket.

Heat the oil in a wok over a high heat, then throw in the spring onions, radishes, carrot, and edamame beans. Stir-fry for 3–4 minutes, then add the chilli, garlic, and Chinese five spice powder and stir-fry for a further minute.

Add the cooked basmati rice and stir-fry for 2–3 minutes until everything has combined.

Remove from the heat and sprinkle over the soy sauce and coriander. Serve immediately.

monday's root vegetable bhuna

I always roast up too many vegetables to go with Sunday lunch. Sometimes accidentally, sometimes intentionally; either way, they make a perfect addition to this simple and spicy bhuna.

Serves 2 generously

1 tbsp sunflower oil

1 onion, peeled and finely chopped

1 red pepper, finely sliced

2 cloves of garlic, peeled and crushed

1 tsp ground cumin

1 tsp ground turmeric

½ tsp dried chilli flakes

1 tbsp medium curry paste (ensure dairy free)

400g (14oz) can chopped tomatoes

2 handfuls of fresh or frozen spinach

½ roasting tray of leftover roasted root vegetables, including carrots, parsnips, red onion, and butternut squash, roughly chopped

Juice of ½ unwaxed lemon

Pinch of sea salt flakes

Heat the oil in a saucepan over a medium–high heat and cook the onion and red pepper for 2 minutes until softened.

Add the garlic, cumin, turmeric, and chilli flakes and cook for a further 1 minute.

Stir in the curry paste and chopped tomatoes, then reduce the heat to medium. Simmer for 8–9 minutes, then stir in the spinach and cook for a further 2 minutes.

Stir in the leftover roasted root vegetables and squeeze over the lemon juice. Season with sea salt.

For the perfect roasted root vegetables, drizzle sunflower oil over peeled carrots, parsnips, quartered red onions, and butternut squash, then roast at 200°C/Gas mark 6 for 35–40 minutes, turning once. Allow the leftovers to cool fully, then refrigerate for use the following day.

Suitable for freezing.

chilli and ginger stir-fried greens

If you struggle to use up the last few vegetables from the back of your fridge, this recipe will transform them into a light meal. Adapt the fresh ingredients to what you have available, and enjoy a new dish each time.

Serves 2

---

1 tbsp sunflower oil

2cm (¾in) piece of ginger, peeled and grated

1 tsp dried chilli flakes

8 florets of Tenderstem broccoli

8 sugar snap peas, halved diagonally

2 handfuls of spring greens, roughly chopped

2 handfuls of kale, stems removed and roughly chopped

2 tbsp roasted cashew nuts

1 spring onion, finely chopped

Juice of ½ unwaxed lime

Generous handful of coriander, roughly torn

It's worth buying fresh ginger for its zingy and warming flavour. Store it in the freezer, gently scrape away the skin, and then grate it from frozen into your dishes. Staying frozen won't affect the flavour and it will keep it fresher for longer.

Heat the oil in a wok over a high heat and cook the ginger and chilli flakes for 1 minute to infuse the oil.

Throw in the broccoli, sugar snap peas, spring greens, and kale and stir-fry for 4–5 minutes, moving the vegetables constantly.

Stir through the cashew nuts and spring onion, then stir-fry for a further minute.

Remove from the heat and squeeze over the lime juice. Scatter with the coriander and serve while hot.

chickpea bunny chow

Bunny chow originates from the Durban area of South Africa, where curries were stuffed into hollowed-out bread loaves to make them a transportable meal. I love using up bread rolls to create open "bowls" for this spiced chickpea curry – the sauce soaks into the bread, keeping the flavours lingering throughout.

Serves 4

2 tbsp sunflower oil

1 onion, peeled and diced

2 cloves of garlic, peeled and crushed

10 green beans, sliced

4 leaves of cavolo nero, stems removed and roughly chopped

1 tsp garam masala

1 tsp mild curry paste (ensure dairy free)

1 tsp mild chilli powder

½ tsp ground turmeric

½ tsp ground cumin

2cm (¾in) piece of ginger, peeled and grated

400g (14oz) can chickpeas, drained and rinsed

4 large crusty bread rolls, halved and hollowed out

Juice of 1 unwaxed lemon

Generous pinch of sea salt flakes

Handful of coriander leaves, roughly torn

Preheat the oven to 180°C/Gas mark 4.

Heat the oil in a large saucepan over a medium–high heat and cook the onion, garlic, green beans, and cavolo nero for 2 minutes.

Spoon in the garam masala, curry paste, chilli powder, turmeric, cumin, and ginger and cook for 5 minutes, stirring frequently. Tip in the chickpeas, stir, and cook for a further 5 minutes.

In the meantime, place the hollowed-out bread rolls on a baking tray and warm in the oven for 5–6 minutes, then set aside.

Remove the pan from the heat, then squeeze in the lemon juice. Season with sea salt and scatter in the coriander. Use a spoon to carefully fill the warm bread rolls with the curry, and serve immediately.

Use the discarded bread to make Panzanella (page 35) or blitz into breadcrumbs and freeze for when you need them.

fiery butternut squash ketchup

As each butternut squash can vary in size, it can be easy to end up with excess roasted butternut squash. Use leftover roasted squash to make this delicious ketchup, which tastes great with Carrot fries with cinnamon salt (page 86).

Makes 1 small pot

150g (5½oz) leftover roasted butternut squash

1 tsp harissa paste

Juice of ¼ unwaxed lemon

Pinch of sea salt flakes

2 tsp plain soya yoghurt

Harissa is a hot, aromatic spice paste made using chillies, spices, herbs, and a little rose water. It is available in most supermarkets and Middle Eastern shops, and keeps for months in the fridge. Use it to add flavour to tagines, soups, and houmous for plenty of heat with little effort.

For the perfect roasted butternut squash, drizzle sunflower oil over the peeled veg, season with salt and pepper, then roast at 200°C/ Gas mark 6 for 35–40 minutes, turning once.

Suitable for freezing.

Add the roasted butternut squash, harissa paste, lemon juice, and sea salt with 100ml (3½fl oz/scant ½ cup) of cold water to a blender, or blend in a bowl with a hand blender and blitz until smooth.

Swirl through the soya yoghurt and serve as a dip.

patatas bravas

This traditional Spanish tapas dish is the perfect way to revive leftover potatoes and create a small sharing plate. Serve alongside Fig and tarragon stuffed pittas (page 91), Gigantes plaki (page 50) and Pantry antipasti salad (page 69).

Serves 4

---

3 tbsp sunflower oil

1 red onion, peeled and finely chopped

3 cloves of garlic, peeled and crushed

2 tsp sweet paprika

1 tsp smoked paprika

1 tsp mild chilli powder

400g (14oz) can chopped tomatoes

½ tsp sugar

300g (10½oz) leftover boiled potatoes, cut into small cubes

Generous pinch of sea salt flakes

Handful of flat-leaf parsley, roughly chopped

1 red chilli, deseeded and finely sliced

If you don't have any leftover boiled potatoes, canned new potatoes work well in this recipe. Simply drain and rinse them thoroughly, so the flavours absorb into the potatoes.

Suitable for freezing.

Heat 1 tablespoon of the oil in a frying pan over a medium–high heat and cook the onion for 2 minutes until softened. Add the garlic, paprikas, and chilli powder, stir, and cook for a further minute.

Tip in the chopped tomatoes and sugar, reduce to a medium heat, and cook for 10 minutes, stirring occasionally.

In the meantime, heat the remaining 2 tablespoons of oil in a separate frying pan over a medium heat and fry the potato cubes for 10 minutes, or until the edges are golden.

Stir the golden potatoes into the spicy tomato sauce. Remove from the heat, then season with sea salt.

Scatter over the parsley and chilli slices just before serving.

cauliflower and broccoli cheese

I love a slow-baked vegan cauliflower cheese, but don't always have the time to make it. This fast recipe uses up cauliflower and broccoli, along with essentials from the fridge and store cupboard to bring you a tasty version in less than 15 minutes. Serve as a side dish, or with a crisp salad for a fast dinner. Vegan cream cheese can be found in most large supermarkets. It's worth trying own brand varieties, to save some money.

Serves 4 as a side dish

½ cauliflower, leaves removed and cut into small florets

½ broccoli, cut into small florets

2 tbsp flaked almonds

4 tbsp vegan cream cheese

200ml (7fl oz/generous ¾ cup) unsweetened soya milk

Small handful of chives, finely chopped

Generous pinch of sea salt flakes

Toasted almonds add crunch and a slow-cooked flavour to this speedy dish.

Steam the cauliflower and broccoli florets for 8–10 minutes until al dente.

In the meantime, add the flaked almonds to a dry frying pan and toast over a high heat for 1–2 minutes until golden. Set aside.

Place a saucepan over a medium heat and add the cream cheese and soya milk. Whisk until combined for 5–6 minutes, then remove from the heat and stir in the chives.

Spoon in the cooked cauliflower and broccoli florets and stir to coat in the sauce. Scatter over the flaked almonds and season with sea salt.

panzanella

A delicious and rustic salad to use up stale bread. I love to use leftover crusty white bread, but thick-sliced or ciabatta is also delicious.

Serves 2

200g (7oz) stale white bread, torn into 4cm (1½in) pieces

400g (14oz) mixed tomatoes, roughly chopped

Generous pinch of sea salt flakes and black pepper

6 tbsp extra virgin olive oil

4 sundried tomatoes in oil, roughly chopped

2 tbsp capers, drained

Generous handful of basil leaves, torn

Good-quality extra virgin olive oil gives a fruity, peppery taste to this salad. Choose the best you can afford, and save it for drizzling and dressing.

Preheat the oven to 160°C/Gas mark 2–3.

Arrange the torn bread on a baking tray, then dry out in the oven for 12 minutes.

In a bowl, season the tomatoes with the sea salt and black pepper, then drizzle with the oil. Stir through the sundried tomatoes and capers, then leave to infuse for 10 minutes.

Stir the warm bread into the tomato mixture and scatter over the basil leaves.

garden crumble

Empty your vegetable drawer into this hearty meal that friends and family will love. If you've never tried a savoury crumble before, you're in for a treat!

Serves 4

1 tbsp sunflower oil

1 onion, peeled and roughly chopped

1 clove of garlic, peeled and crushed

1 medium courgette, diced

1 red pepper, sliced

6 cherry tomatoes, halved

10 green beans, sliced

1 tsp herbes de Provence

1 tsp dried rosemary

400g (14oz) can chopped tomatoes

Generous pinch of sea salt flakes and black pepper

For the crumble topping
100g (3½oz) plain flour

50g (1¾oz) rolled oats

2 tbsp shelled walnuts, roughly chopped

2 tbsp vegan butter

Zest of 1 unwaxed lemon

Preheat the oven to 200°C/Gas mark 6.

Heat the oil in a large saucepan over a medium–high heat and cook the onion for 2 minutes until softened. Add the garlic, courgette, red pepper, cherry tomatoes, and green beans and sprinkle in the herbes de Provence and rosemary. Cook for a further 2 minutes, then tip in the chopped tomatoes, and season with the sea salt and black pepper. Simmer for 10 minutes.

In the meantime, make the crumble topping. Mix the flour, oats, and walnuts in a bowl, then rub in the vegan butter until the mixture resembles breadcrumbs. Stir through the lemon zest, then spoon evenly onto a baking sheet. Bake for 8–9 minutes until golden.

Spoon the vegetable mixture into a serving dish, then sprinkle over the crumble topping just before serving.

Adding chopped walnuts to the topping gives extra crunch and a toasted flavour. It also works well with pumpkin seeds, sunflower seeds, and mixed chopped nuts.

apple and fennel salad with orange and black pepper

This simple salad is the perfect way to use the last of the apples. I love it as a peppery side to the Butterbean, lemon, and kale one-pot (page 127).

Serves 2

---

2 tbsp walnuts, roughly chopped

1 small fennel bulb, finely sliced

2 green apples, finely sliced

2 sticks of celery, finely sliced

2 generous handfuls of rocket

Juice of ½ unwaxed orange

Generous pinch of black pepper

Fennel bulbs can often be found in the reduced section of supermarket chillers. It's delicious served raw in this salad, or slowly roasted with tomatoes for 30–40 minutes at 180°C/Gas mark 4.

Add the walnuts to a dry frying pan and toast over a high heat for 1–2 minutes.

Combine the fennel, apples, celery, and rocket in a bowl. Squeeze over the orange juice and sprinkle with black pepper. Combine again.

Top with the toasted walnuts.

sweet chilli sauce

I buy bags of chillies with good intentions of throwing them into stir-fries, scattering them over noodles, and giving heat to curries, but always struggle to use up the last few. This Thai-style sweet chilli sauce is excellent for dipping, adding to dressings and, of course, gifting to a loved one.

Makes 1 large jar

3 red chillies

4 cloves of garlic, peeled

Small handful of coriander leaves

Zest of 1 unwaxed lime

200g (7oz) granulated sugar

1 rounded tbsp cornflour

100ml (3½fl oz/scant ½ cup) white wine vinegar

Chillies vary in heat intensity. Remove the seeds and pith if you want a milder sauce, or leave them in for a hotter experience.

Blitz the chillies, garlic, coriander and lime zest in a food processor, or finely chop and combine.

Add the chilli mix to a frying pan with the sugar, cornflour, and 250ml (8¾fl oz/1 cup) of cold water. Bring to the boil over a high heat, then reduce to a simmer for 10 minutes, stirring frequently.

Pour in the vinegar and simmer for a further 3 minutes. Allow to cool, then pour into a clean, airtight jar.

pea guacamole toasts

Avocado toast makes for a delicious brunch, but let's face it, avocados are an expensive ingredient to purchase frequently. This guacamole uses frozen peas in place of avocado for a fresh, cost-effective brunch.

Serves 2

200g (7oz) frozen peas

1 small red onion, peeled and finely chopped

1 tomato, deseeded and chopped

Small handful of coriander leaves, finely chopped

Juice of 1 unwaxed lime

Generous pinch of sea salt flakes

2 slices of thick white toast

I love a chunky guacamole, but if you prefer a smoother spread, simply blitz the peas in a blender before adding the other ingredients.

Defrost and simmer the peas in a saucepan of hot water for 2–3 minutes, then drain and tip the peas into a mixing bowl.

Use a potato masher to crush the peas until semi-smooth, then stir in the onion, tomato, and coriander.

Stir in the lime juice and mix until combined. Season with sea salt.

Load generously onto hot toast.

pan-roasted balsamic vegetable baguettes

This tasty and substantial lunch can be made with the vegetables left at the end of the week, pan-roasted with balsamic vinegar for a Mediterranean flavour.

Serves 2

1 tbsp sunflower oil

¼ tsp dried oregano

1 courgette, sliced

1 yellow pepper, deseeded and sliced

1 red onion, peeled and quartered

6 cherry tomatoes

2 small white baguettes

2 tbsp balsamic vinegar

Look out for reduced-price baguettes from supermarkets and bakeries, or keep some par-baked baguettes in your cupboard for a quick, hot sandwich.

Preheat the oven to 160°C/Gas mark 2–3.

Heat the oil and oregano in a large frying pan over a medium heat. Add the courgette, yellow pepper, onion, and cherry tomatoes and cook for 5–6 minutes, stirring frequently.

In the meantime, place the baguettes in the oven to warm for 5–6 minutes.

When the vegetables have begun to soften, add the balsamic vinegar and cook to reduce for 2 minutes.

Remove the warm baguettes from the oven and carefully cut open. Generously spoon the hot vegetables into the baguettes and serve immediately.

grilled pepper fajitas

Revive those wrinkly peppers with this family-friendly recipe. Fajita spice mixes can be expensive, so make your own using spices that are already in your cupboard - make a big batch so you always have some to hand.

Serves 2

2 tbsp sunflower oil

1 red pepper, deseeded and cut into 3cm (1¼in) slices

1 yellow pepper, deseeded and cut into 3cm (1¼in) slices

2 red onions, peeled and finely sliced

400g (14oz) can red kidney beans, drained and rinsed

For the seasoning mix
1 tbsp mild chilli powder

1 tsp smoked paprika

½ tsp garlic powder

½ tsp ground cumin

½ tsp fine sea salt

To serve
2–4 soft tortilla wraps, warmed

1 baby gem lettuce, roughly cut into wedges

2 tbsp vegan cream cheese

Small handful of coriander, torn

Juice of ½ unwaxed lime

Brush a griddle pan with 1 tablespoon of the oil and heat over a medium–high heat.

Use tongs to carefully place the pepper slices onto the hot griddle pan. Allow to sizzle for 5 minutes, turn to the other side, and griddle for a further 3 minutes until grill marks appear.

Heat the remaining tablespoon of oil in a wok or large frying pan over a medium–high heat and add the red onions and red kidney beans, along with the chilli powder, smoked paprika, garlic powder, ground cumin, and sea salt, and stir-fry for 5 minutes until fragrant and the beans are coated in the spices. Remove from the heat.

Carefully transfer the grilled peppers from the griddle pan into the wok. Stir to combine.

Fill the warmed tortilla wraps with the cooked vegetables and beans, then add the lettuce, cream cheese, and coriander. Squeeze over the lime juice and fold the wraps.

Soft tortilla wraps freeze well and defrost within a few minutes, so store them in the freezer and take out the amount you need to avoid waste.

FROM THE
CUPBOARD

gigantes plaki

These Greek-style beans are usually slow baked, but I love this quick recipe that will have them on the table within 15 minutes. Serve hot with crusty bread or sliced potatoes, or allow them to cool and enjoy as part of a mezze with Moroccan-spiced flatbreads (page 53).

Serves 2 as a main

---

1 tbsp sunflower oil

1 onion, peeled and finely chopped

1 stick of celery, finely diced

1 carrot, peeled and finely chopped

1 clove of garlic, peeled and crushed

1 tsp sweet paprika

1 tsp dried oregano

½ tsp mild chilli powder

½ tsp ground cinnamon

400g (14oz) can chopped tomatoes

1 tsp granulated sugar

400g (14oz) can butter beans, drained and rinsed

2 tbsp tomato ketchup

Generous handful of flat-leaf parsley, finely chopped

Small handful of mint leaves, finely chopped

Generous pinch of sea salt flakes

Heat the oil in a large saucepan over a medium–high heat and cook the onion, celery, and carrot for 2–3 minutes until beginning to soften.

Add the garlic, paprika, oregano, chilli powder, and cinnamon and cook for a further minute.

Pour in the tomatoes, sugar, butter beans, and ketchup, then reduce the heat to medium. Cook for 10 minutes, stirring frequently.

Remove the pan from the heat, then stir through the parsley and mint. Season with sea salt.

Don't skimp on fresh herbs for this recipe! The freshness is what makes gigantes plaki unique. Save time by chopping the herbs while the other ingredients are cooking.

Suitable for freezing.

moroccan-spiced flatbreads

Don't waste money on flavoured flatbreads. Use store-cupboard spices to liven up plain flatbreads with this Middle Eastern-inspired flavour infusion. Enjoy with the Spinach, chickpea and lemon pilaf (page 58).

Serves 4

2 tbsp olive oil

¼ tsp ground cumin

¼ tsp ground ginger

¼ tsp ground allspice

¼ tsp mild chilli powder

Zest of 1 unwaxed lemon

4 large flatbreads (ensure dairy free)

1 tbsp sultanas

Small handful of flat-leaf parsley leaves, roughly chopped

Pinch of sea salt flakes

This spice mix also works well on pitta breads.

Preheat the oven to 180°C/Gas mark 4.

In a small bowl, mix together the oil, cumin, ginger, allspice, chilli powder, and lemon zest until combined.

Arrange the flatbreads on a baking tray. Brush over a thin coat of the spiced oil using a pastry brush, then sprinkle over the sultanas.

Bake for 8–10 minutes until hot and golden, then scatter with the parsley and sea salt.

laksa noodles

The perfect weekend lunch – fast and on a budget! These noodles strike the perfect balance of heat, spice, creaminess, and zest. Find coconut milk cheaper in the world food aisle of large supermarkets, or opt for own brand varieties which are considerably cheaper than branded versions.

Serves 2 generously

---

1 tbsp sunflower oil

2 red chillies, deseeded and chopped

2cm (¾in) piece of ginger, peeled and grated

3 cloves of garlic, peeled and crushed

1 tsp Chinese five-spice powder

1 tbsp light soy sauce

4 spring onions, finely chopped

1 carrot, peeled and roughly sliced

6 sugar snap peas, halved diagonally

1 red pepper, deseeded and finely sliced

400ml (14fl oz) can coconut milk

1 tbsp smooth peanut butter

300g (10½oz) ready-to-wok soft noodles (ensure egg free)

Juice of ½ unwaxed lime

Handful of coriander leaves, roughly torn

Heat the oil in a large wok over a medium heat, then throw in the chillies, ginger, garlic, Chinese five spice, soy sauce, and 3 of the spring onions. Stir-fry for 2 minutes to infuse the oil.

Increase the heat to high and throw in the carrot, sugar snap peas, and red pepper, then stir-fry for further 2 minutes.

Pour in the coconut milk and stir through the peanut butter. Stir to combine and simmer for 5 minutes, stirring frequently.

Carefully add the noodles, stir, and cook for a further 4 minutes.

Remove from the heat and squeeze over the lime juice. Scatter with the coriander leaves and the remaining spring onion. Serve immediately.

Ready-to-wok noodles are great to keep in your store cupboard for a fast addition to stir-fries or eastern-style curries. Ensure they are egg free, or try soft rice noodles.

spanish chickpea stew

Transport yourself to the Mediterranean with this store-cupboard stew. The recipe uses frozen spinach, but works equally well with fresh spinach, if you have it available.

Serves 2 generously

---

1 tbsp sunflower oil

1 onion, peeled and finely diced

1 carrot, peeled and diced

2 cloves of garlic, peeled and sliced

1 yellow pepper, deseeded and finely sliced

2 tsp sweet smoked paprika

1 tsp smoked paprika

½ tsp dried chilli flakes

½ tsp ground cumin

½ tsp dried thyme

400g (14oz) can chopped tomatoes

400g (14oz) can chickpeas, drained and rinsed

Pinch of granulated sugar

10 black olives, pitted

2 handfuls of frozen or fresh spinach

Generous handful of flat-leaf parsley, finely chopped

Juice of ½ unwaxed lemon

Generous pinch of sea salt flakes

Heat the oil in a large saucepan over a medium–high heat and cook the onion and carrot for 2 minutes until they begin to soften.

Add the garlic, yellow pepper, sweet and smoked paprikas, chilli flakes, cumin, and thyme and stir for 2 minutes until coated in the spices.

Pour in the chopped tomatoes and chickpeas, then stir in the sugar. Simmer for 8 minutes, stirring occasionally.

Stir through the olives and spinach and cook for a further 2 minutes.

Remove from the heat and stir through the parsley. Squeeze over the lemon juice and season with sea salt.

Finely chop the flat-leaf parsley while the stew is simmering, to save time at the end.

Suitable for freezing.

middle eastern harira

This fragrant soup is substantial enough to enjoy for dinner, when you're looking for a light, balanced meal in a bowl. No passata available? Blend canned chopped tomatoes until smooth.

Serves 4

2 tbsp sunflower oil

3 cloves of garlic, peeled and crushed

1 tsp ground turmeric

1 tsp ground cumin

½ tsp ground cinnamon

2 carrots, peeled and roughly chopped

1 stick of celery, roughly chopped

1 red chilli, deseeded and sliced

500g (1lb 2oz) passata

1.5 litres (2½ pints) hot vegetable stock

400g (14oz) can green lentils, drained and rinsed

400g (14oz) can chickpeas, drained and rinsed

1 tbsp flaked almonds

Generous handful of flat-leaf parsley, finely chopped

Generous handful of coriander leaves, roughly torn

Zest and juice of 1 unwaxed lemon

Pinch of sea salt flakes

Heat the oil in a large saucepan over a medium heat and cook the garlic, turmeric, cumin, and cinnamon for 1 minute to infuse the oil.

Add the carrots, celery, and chilli and cook for a further 3 minutes until beginning to soften.

Pour in the passata, vegetable stock, green lentils, and chickpeas and simmer for 10 minutes, stirring occasionally.

In the meantime, add the flaked almonds to a dry frying pan and toast over a high heat for 3–4 minutes until golden, then tip onto kitchen paper.

Remove the soup from the heat and stir through the parsley, coriander, and lemon zest. Squeeze in the lemon juice and season with sea salt. Garnish with the toasted almonds just before serving.

There's no need to blend this soup as the varying textures are delicious!

Suitable for freezing.

spinach, chickpea, and lemon pilaf

Try this simple one-pot dish for a warming lunch, or serve it cold as a sharing side dish.

Serves 4

1 tbsp sunflower oil

1 red onion, peeled and finely chopped

1 tsp ground turmeric

1 tsp ground cumin

1 tsp garam masala

¼ tsp dried chilli flakes

250g (9oz) basmati rice

600ml (1 pint/2½ cups) hot vegetable stock

400g (14oz) can chickpeas, drained and rinsed

4 generous handfuls of spinach leaves

Juice of 1 unwaxed lemon

Generous handful of coriander leaves, finely chopped

Generous pinch of sea salt flakes

Frozen spinach also works well in this dish, if you have no fresh spinach available. If using frozen, add it in step 2, to cook with the rice and stock.

Heat the oil in a large saucepan over a medium–high heat and cook the onion for 2 minutes until softened but not browned. Add the turmeric, cumin, garam masala, and chilli flakes and stir through for 1 minute.

Pour in the rice and vegetable stock, reduce the heat to medium, then simmer for 8 minutes, stirring frequently to avoid the rice sticking.

Add the chickpeas and spinach and cook for a further 2 minutes.

Remove from the heat and stir through the lemon juice and coriander. Season with sea salt.

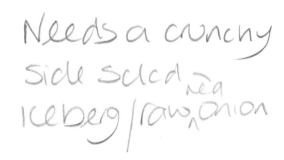

Needs a crunchy side salad ~eg iceberg / raw onion

crispy leek gratin

Although it tastes slow cooked, this fast gratin makes an ideal side dish or lunch for two with a leafy, green salad. I love serving this with Baked bean and sage pie (page 130) for a family dinner. Try supermarket own brand vegan cream cheese in this recipe, available in most large supermarkets - it costs less than the branded varieties, and you'll notice very little difference in taste.

Serves 2 generously

---

4 tbsp rolled oats

1 tbsp pumpkin seeds

1 tbsp sunflower seeds

Generous pinch of sea salt

1 tbsp sunflower oil

2 large leeks, finely chopped

2 cloves of garlic, peeled and crushed

150ml (5fl oz/generous ½ cup) unsweetened soya milk

4 tbsp vegan cream cheese

Cooking the topping separately to the creamy leeks ensures a speedy cooking time.

Preheat the oven to 200°C/Gas mark 6.

Spread the oats, pumpkin seeds, and sunflower seeds evenly on a baking tray. Season with sea salt, then bake for 8–10 minutes until golden.

In the meantime, heat the oil in a large frying pan over a medium–high heat and cook the leeks for 7 minutes until soft. Reduce the heat to medium, then add the garlic and cook for a further minute. Pour in the soya milk and vegan cream cheese and simmer for 5 minutes. Stir frequently to distribute the cheese and ensure even melting.

Pour the leek mixture into a serving dish, then scatter with the toasted oats and seeds. Serve hot.

10-minute perfect pasta sauce

Tomato pasta can be all you need for a good meal. This homemade sauce is tastier than a jar of shop-bought sauce. Make in bulk and freeze for easy weekday meals.

Serves 4

1 tbsp sunflower oil

2 cloves of garlic, peeled and crushed

½ tsp dried chilli flakes (optional)

400g (14oz) passata

½ tsp granulated sugar

Generous pinch of sea salt flakes and black pepper

Heat the oil in a saucepan over a medium heat and cook the garlic for 1 minute until softened, then add the chilli flakes and cook for a further minute, stirring to avoid sticking. (The addition of dried chilli flakes gives a little heat to this sauce, but it is also delicious without.)

Stir in the passata and sugar, then simmer for 10 minutes.

Remove from the heat and season well with sea salt and black pepper.

sweetcorn salsa

This two-step salsa brightens up any table! Serve with tortilla chips or veggie chilli, or load into Chilli bean sliders (page 119).

Serves 4

325g (11oz) canned sweetcorn, drained and rinsed

1 red pepper, deseeded and finely diced

1 small red onion, peeled and finely chopped

2 tomatoes, deseeded and chopped

Handful of coriander, finely chopped

Small handful of flat-leaf parsley, finely chopped

Juice of 1 unwaxed lime

Generous pinch of smoked sea salt flakes

In a bowl, combine the sweetcorn, red pepper, onion, tomatoes, coriander, and parsley.

Squeeze over the lime juice and season with smoked salt.

Smoked salt adds a subtle layer of flavour to the salsa, but if you don't have any available, regular sea salt works fine.

thai slaw

Give your classic coleslaw an Eastern twist. Store-cupboard ingredients make a no-cook sauce, which is delicious with crunchy, raw vegetables. Also delicious with Soy-roasted broccoli green curry (page 101).

Serves 4

---

4 tbsp smooth peanut butter

1 tbsp dark soy sauce

1 red chilli, deseeded and finely chopped

1 spring onion, finely sliced

2 carrots, peeled and finely sliced

1 red pepper, deseeded and finely sliced

1 red onion, peeled and finely sliced

1 green apple, cored and finely sliced

¼ small red cabbage, finely shredded

The oil content in peanut butter varies from brand to brand, so you may need to add a little more water in the sauce. Add it 1 tablespoon at a time, until the sauce evenly coats the back of the spoon.

In a mixing bowl, whisk together the peanut butter and soy sauce with 100ml (3½fl oz/scant ½ cup) of cold water until smooth. Stir through the chilli and spring onion.

In a serving bowl, toss together the carrots, red pepper, onion, green apple, and cabbage.

Pour over the peanut sauce and stir until the vegetables are evenly coated.

caribbean sweet potato and coconut soup

This silken soup tastes as if it has been slow cooked, with a warming spice blend, rich coconut milk, and fragrant herbs. The key to cooking this soup in 15 minutes is grating the sweet potato. This exposes more surface area to the heat, therefore creating a faster cooking time. It's all in the science!

Serves 4

---

2 tbsp sunflower oil

2 sweet potatoes, peeled and grated

1 onion, peeled and diced

1 yellow pepper, deseeded and roughly chopped

2 tsp jerk seasoning

400ml (14fl oz) can coconut milk

800ml (scant 1½ pints/3½ cups) hot vegetable stock

Generous handful of coriander leaves, some reserved for garnishing

Juice of 1 unwaxed lime

Pinch of sea salt flakes and black pepper

Jerk seasoning is a pre-blended spice mix of ground chillies, thyme, allspice, cinnamon, and hot cayenne pepper. It's great to keep in the cupboard for easy Jamaican-style curries, or to sprinkle over oven-cooked chips for a fiery flavour twist.

Suitable for freezing.

Heat the oil in a large saucepan over a medium–high heat and cook the sweet potatoes, onion, yellow pepper, and jerk seasoning for 3–4 minutes, stirring constantly, until the onion has begun to soften.

Pour in the coconut milk and vegetable stock, and loosely cover with a lid. Simmer for 10 minutes, then remove from the heat.

Stir in the coriander leaves, then blend until completely smooth using a hand blender or jug blender.

Squeeze in the lime juice and season with sea salt and black pepper. Garnish with coriander leaves just before serving.

golden couscous with apricots and mint

bulgur wheat ~~orange~~

Transform dried couscous into a fragrant and flavourful plate that the whole family will love. There's no need to buy expensive pre-packed couscous salads when it's so quick, easy, and cheap to make your own.

Serves 4 generously

500g (1lb 2oz) dried couscous

1 tsp ground turmeric

½ tsp ground cinnamon

500ml (17½fl oz/2 cups) hot vegetable stock

150g (5½oz) dried apricots, roughly chopped

1 tbsp sunflower oil

400g (14oz) can chickpeas, drained and rinsed

Zest and juice of 1 unwaxed lemon

Generous drizzle of extra virgin olive oil

Generous handful of mint leaves, finely chopped

Generous handful of flat-leaf parsley, finely chopped

Generous pinch of sea salt

Bring the lemon to room temperature to get more juice from the fruit.

In a large bowl, stir together the couscous, turmeric, cinnamon, vegetable stock, and apricots. Cover with a plate and allow the couscous to steam for 10 minutes.

In the meantime, heat the sunflower oil in a saucepan over a medium–high heat. Add the chickpeas and cook for 8–9 minutes, stirring frequently until golden brown.

Fork through the couscous to separate the grains, then add the lemon juice and zest. Stir through the olive oil, mint, and parsley. Season with sea salt.

Spoon into a large serving bowl and make a small well in the middle. Spoon in the chickpeas and serve.

the big pizza pot

When the need for pizza arises but you don't have the time to make a base, whip up this 15-minute casserole that has all the flavours of pizza. If you have vegan cheese available, grate a little over just before serving with slices of garlic bread.

Serves 4

---

1 tbsp sunflower oil

1 onion, peeled and roughly chopped

1 clove of garlic, peeled and finely sliced

1 tsp dried oregano

½ tsp dried mixed herbs

1 green pepper, deseeded and roughly sliced

10 closed-cup mushrooms, sliced

400g (14oz) can chopped tomatoes

4 sundried tomatoes in oil, drained and sliced

10 black olives, pitted and halved

100g (3½oz) canned, frozen or fresh pineapple chunks

2 tbsp frozen or canned sweetcorn

1 tbsp tomato ketchup

Generous pinch of sea flakes and black pepper

Generous handful of basil leaves

Heat the oil in a large saucepan over a medium–high heat and cook the onion and garlic for 2 minutes until softened but not browned. Sprinkle in the oregano and mixed herbs.

Add the green pepper and mushrooms and cook for a further 2 minutes, stirring constantly.

Pour in the chopped tomatoes along with the sundried tomatoes, olives, pineapple chunks, and sweetcorn. Stir in the tomato ketchup and reduce the heat to medium. Simmer for 10 minutes.

Remove from the heat and season with sea salt and black pepper. Scatter with the basil leaves just before serving.

The big pizza pot freezes well for up to three months.

butter bean houmous

If you like your houmous creamy and whipped, switch chickpeas for budget-friendly butter beans in this twist on the classic dip.

Makes 1 small pot

400g (14oz) can butter beans, drained and rinsed

2 tbsp tahini

Juice of 1 unwaxed lemon

6 tbsp extra virgin olive oil

1 clove of garlic, peeled

Pinch of sea salt

Generous handful of flat-leaf parsley, finely chopped

Smooth peanut butter makes a great substitute for tahini (a sesame seed paste) if you don't have any available. Just add a little extra oil at the blending stage.

Place the butter beans, tahini, and lemon juice in a food processor or blender jug and blitz until semi-smooth.

Add 5 tablespoons of the oil, the garlic and sea salt, and blitz again until smooth.

Stir the flat-leaf parsley through the houmous, along with the remaining tablespoon of oil.

pantry antipasti salad

I love having a few jars of antipasti vegetables in oil stored in the cupboard, ready to add to a pizza, casserole, sandwich – or this four-step salad. Toasted walnuts, almonds or chopped mixed nuts make an excellent alternative to pine nuts, if you don't have them available.

Serves 4 as a side dish

---

1 tbsp pine nuts

100g (3½oz) salad leaves, including spinach and red chard

4 cherry tomatoes, halved

5 sundried tomatoes in oil, drained and roughly chopped

4 artichokes in oil, drained and halved

4 chargrilled peppers in oil, drained and roughly chopped

8 green olives, pitted

Juice of ¼ lemon

Small handful of flat-leaf parsley, finely chopped

Toasting the pine nuts gives a sweeter flavour and addictive crunch.

Toast the pine nuts in a dry pan over a high heat for 2 minutes, then tip onto kitchen paper.

Toss the salad leaves with the cherry tomatoes in a bowl, then stir through the sundried tomatoes, artichokes, peppers and olives.

Squeeze over the lemon juice and scatter with the parsley.

Sprinkle over the toasted pine nuts.

lebanese lentils, rice, and caramelized onions

Simple, delicious, budget-friendly comfort food that will become a classic in your kitchen.

Serves 4

180g (6oz) basmati rice

2 tbsp sunflower oil

3 large red onions, peeled and finely sliced

2 tsp soft brown sugar

½ tsp ground cumin

½ tsp ground cinnamon

½ tsp ground turmeric

½ tsp mild chilli powder

400g (14oz) can green lentils, drained and rinsed

Small handful of flat-leaf parsley, roughly chopped

2 tbsp unsweetened soya yoghurt

Juice of ¼ unwaxed lemon

Generous pinch of sea salt flakes

This dish is also delicious served chilled as a sharing pilaf.

In a large saucepan, add the basmati rice and cover with cold water. Bring to the boil over a medium–high heat for 12 minutes, stirring occasionally, until the water is absorbed and the rice appears fluffy, then set aside.

In the meantime, heat the oil in a large frying pan over a high heat and cook the onions for 5 minutes, then add the brown sugar and cook for a further 5 minutes until caramelized, stirring frequently.

Add the cumin, cinnamon, turmeric, and chilli powder to the onions, then cook for a further minute.

Tip the spiced onions and any remaining oil into the rice, along with the lentils. Return to the heat and stir through for 1 minute.

Scatter over the parsley and divide into warmed bowls. Spoon on the soya yoghurt, squeeze over the lemon juice and season with sea salt.

black-eyed bean mole

I can't get enough of this cocoa-infused mole that uses store cupboard ingredients to create a warming meal. It's great as a weeknight Mexican supper!

Serves 4

1 tbsp sunflower oil

2 red chillies, deseeded and sliced

1 onion, peeled and finely chopped

1 green pepper, deseeded and finely sliced

1 clove of garlic, peeled and crushed

1 tsp mild chilli powder

½ tsp ground cinnamon

400g (14oz) can chopped tomatoes

1 tbsp tomato ketchup

2 tsp cocoa powder

~~Pinch of granulated sugar~~

400g (14oz) can black-eyed beans, drained and rinsed

Small handful of coriander leaves, roughly torn *& peas or leaves*

Pinch of smoked sea salt flakes

Heat the oil in a large saucepan over a medium heat and cook the chillies, onion, green pepper, and garlic for 3 minutes until the onion begins to soften but not brown.

Add the chilli powder and cinnamon and stir through.

Pour in the chopped tomatoes, tomato ketchup, cocoa, sugar, and black-eyed beans, then simmer for 10 minutes, stirring frequently to avoid sticking.

Remove from the heat and scatter over the coriander. Season with smoked sea salt.

& tortilla chips (few) or pasta (½ pot)
~~& nachos~~
& crunchy salad

Serve with Cajun-spiced potatoes (page 100) or a side of rice.

Suitable for freezing.

orzo with peas, mint and parsley pesto

This 10-minute meal is a fast alternative to the classic Italian dish risi e bisi. Instead of using arborio rice, switch to rice-shaped orzo pasta for a comforting bowl of goodness.

Serves 2

250g (9oz) orzo pasta (ensure egg free)

500ml (17½fl oz/2 cups) hot vegetable stock

4 tbsp frozen peas

6 mint leaves, finely chopped

Generous pinch of sea salt flakes and black pepper

For the parsley pesto
30g (1oz) flat-leaf parsley, including the stalks

1 clove of garlic, peeled

2 tbsp flaked almonds

80ml (2½fl oz/⅓ cup) extra virgin olive oil

Parsley has flavour all through its stalk, so use all of the herb in the pesto, not just the leaves.

Put the orzo and vegetable stock in a large saucepan and simmer for 10 minutes until softened and the stock has been absorbed.

In the meantime, make the parsley pesto. Add the parsley, garlic, almonds, and oil to a food processor or blender, and blitz to form a coarse paste. Alternatively, finely chop the ingredients and combine.

Stir the peas and mint into the cooked orzo, and cook for a further 2 minutes.

Remove from the heat and stir through the parsley pesto, then season with sea salt and black pepper.

savoury pancakes with garlicky mushrooms

A simple, thrifty, yet luxurious dinner that transforms basic ingredients into a hearty meal. Why wait until Shrove Tuesday to flip the pancake pan? Soya single cream is cost effective and available in most supermarkets. The UHT varieties tend to be cheaper, and last for longer before use.

Serves 2 generously
(makes about 6)

For the pancakes
100g (3½oz) plain flour

200ml (7fl oz/generous ¾ cup) unsweetened soya milk, chilled

Generous pinch of fine sea salt

6 tbsp sunflower oil

For the garlicky mushrooms
1 tbsp sunflower oil

200g (7oz) button mushrooms, some sliced, some whole

3 cloves of garlic, peeled and finely sliced

6 tbsp soya single cream

Small handful of flat-leaf parsley, finely chopped

Generous pinch of sea salt and black pepper

A handheld balloon whisk is a cheap, essential tool for your utensil drawer, and it mixes the smoothest pancake batter.

Start by making the pancakes. Whisk together the flour, soya milk, and sea salt in a bowl until smooth.

Heat 1 tbsp oil in a frying pan over a medium heat. Test if the oil is hot by adding a drop of pancake batter to the pan: if it sizzles and becomes golden within 30 seconds, it is at optimum temperature. Add 4 tablespoons of the batter to make one pancake and swirl the batter around the pan to coat the base evenly.

When the pancake is golden after 2–3 minutes, carefully flip it over to cook the other side. Drain on kitchen paper then keep warm in the oven while you continue to cook the other pancakes, using 1 tbsp of the oil each time.

For the garlicky mushrooms, heat the oil in a separate frying pan over a medium–high heat and cook the mushrooms for 5 minutes, stirring frequently.

Add the garlic and cook for a further minute. Remove from the heat and stir in the soya cream and parsley. Season with sea salt and black pepper.

To assemble, place the pancakes on serving plates and generously load on the garlicky mushrooms. Fold the pancakes over and serve while hot.

beer-battered onion rings

These pub-style onion rings make a great sharing starter using store cupboard ingredients.

Serves 4

500ml (17½fl oz/2 cups) sunflower oil, for frying

150g (5½oz) self-raising flour

160ml (5½fl oz/generous ½ cup) beer (ensure vegan)

2 large onions, peeled, finely sliced and separated into rings

If you don't have beer available, sparking water makes a similarly light batter, with a less malted flavour.

Heat the oil in a large frying pan over a low–medium heat while you prepare the batter.

In a large bowl, whisk together the flour and beer to form a smooth batter.

Working in batches so you don't overcrowd the pan, dip the rings of onion into the batter, then use tongs to carefully drop them into the hot oil. Cook for 3–4 minutes, or until golden. Carefully remove with tongs or a slotted spoon, then drain on kitchen paper. Serve hot.

pappa al pomodoro

For this classic Tuscan bread and tomato soup, combine canned chopped tomatoes with fresh tomatoes for an authentic sweetness. Unlike ribollita, the bread is added at the end of cooking, so it remains in chunky pieces, like rustic croutons! It's worth using olive oil in this recipe for a fruity depth, but sunflower oil will work well, if that's what you have available.

Serves 2 generously

---

2 thick slices of crusty white bread, roughly torn into chunks

3 tbsp olive oil

3 cloves of garlic, peeled and finely sliced

Pinch of dried chilli flakes

10 cherry tomatoes, halved

400g (14oz) can chopped tomatoes

500ml (17½fl oz/2 cups) hot vegetable stock

½ tsp granulated sugar

Generous pinch of sea salt flakes and black pepper

Handful of basil leaves

Crusts of bread work well for this recipe, and it saves any waste from your loaf!

Suitable for freezing.

Preheat the oven to 180°C/Gas mark 4.

Arrange the chunks of bread on a baking tray and drizzle with 2 tablespoons of the oil. Bake for 8–10 minutes until lightly crisp.

In the meantime, heat the remaining tablespoon of oil in a large saucepan over a medium heat. Cook the garlic, chilli, and cherry tomatoes for 2 minutes until the tomatoes begin to soften.

Pour in the chopped tomatoes and vegetable stock, then sprinkle in the sugar. Stir and simmer for 10 minutes, stirring occasionally, then remove from the heat.

Remove the bread from the oven, then drop it into the soup.

Season with sea salt flakes and black pepper, and scatter with the basil leaves just before serving. Serve either hot or chilled.

two-minute bbq mayonnaise

No need to buy expensive flavoured mayonnaise when you have all the ingredients in the cupboard already! Once exclusive to health food shops, egg-free mayonnaise is now available in most supermarkets, usually in the free-from aisle.

Makes 1 small pot

6 tbsp egg-free mayonnaise (ensure vegan)

2 tbsp BBQ sauce (ensure vegan)

3–4 drops of Tabasco sauce

Juice of ¼ unwaxed lime

Small handful of chives, finely chopped

Serve as a dip with Beer-battered onion rings (page 77).

Add the vegan mayonnaise, BBQ sauce, Tabasco sauce, and lime juice to a bowl and whisk until combined.

Stir through the chives.

FRESH

aubergine caponata

This simple recipe from Sicily combines both fresh and store cupboard ingredients to create a delicious lunch or starter. Traditionally, it is served at room temperature, but it also tastes excellent when hot. Serve this sweet-and-sour dish with warm ciabatta bread.

Serves 2 generously

---

2 tbsp sunflower oil

1 aubergine, chopped into 3cm (1¼in) cubes

1 tsp dried oregano

1 red onion, peeled and finely sliced

1 clove of garlic, peeled and finely sliced

8 cherry tomatoes

1 tbsp sultanas

1 tbsp balsamic vinegar

10 green olives, pitted and halved

Juice of ¼ unwaxed lemon

Generous handful of basil leaves

Pinch of sea salt flakes

For a more substantial dish, or to stretch it to serve more people, add a can of drained and rinsed cannellini beans.

Heat the oil in a large frying pan over a high heat and cook the aubergine and oregano for 5 minutes until starting to soften.

Reduce the heat to medium–high, then add the onion and garlic and cook for 2 minutes.

Add the cherry tomatoes, sultanas, and balsamic vinegar, stir through and cook to reduce for 5 minutes, then stir through the olives.

Remove from the heat and squeeze in the lemon juice. Scatter with the basil leaves and sea salt just before serving.

four-ingredient soured cream with chives

Load this vegan soured cream over the Tortilla tacos (page 132), for a tangy flavour experience.

Makes 1 small pot

---

8 tbsp unsweetened soya yoghurt

Juice of ¼ unwaxed lemon

Pinch of sea salt

Small handful of chives, finely chopped

In a bowl, whisk together the soya yoghurt and lemon juice until combined. Refrigerate for 10 minutes.

Sprinkle in the sea salt and whisk again. Stir through the chives.

Opt for unsweetened, plain soya yoghurt for this recipe. You can use the rest to make a curry extra creamy, or make your own flavoured sweet yoghurt with fruits you have available.

broccoli pesto

Boost your pesto with the addition of broccoli! It will also stretch the pesto further to make it a wonderful pasta sauce to serve four. If you don't have a food processor or blender, you can finely chop or grate all the ingredients before mixing into a coarse pesto.

Makes 1 pot

---

1 tbsp flaked almonds

1 large broccoli, cut into florets

1 small handful of basil, including the stalks

Juice of ½ unwaxed lemon

1 clove of garlic, peeled

4 tbsp extra virgin olive oil

½ tsp sea salt

In a dry frying pan, toast the flaked almonds over a high heat for 2 minutes until golden, then tip them into a food processor or blender.

Add the broccoli florets, basil, lemon juice, garlic, and oil and blitz to a coarse paste. Stir through the sea salt.

Don't waste the broccoli stalk – chop it finely and add it to a stir-fry for a fresh, crunchy addition.

Suitable for freezing.

corn on the cob with chilli and lime

Bring the taste of summer to your kitchen any time of the year. I love this
grilled, tender, and zesty corn on the cob, which is made absolutely perfect
by the addition of smoked sea salt, which you'll find in most supermarkets.

Serves 2 as a side dish

2 corn on the cob, leaves
removed

2 tbsp olive oil

1 tsp dried chilli flakes

Juice of ¼ unwaxed lime

Generous pinch of smoked sea
salt flakes

Small handful of coriander
leaves, finely chopped

Frozen corn on the cob also works
well in this recipe, meaning you
can enjoy it out of season for a
cheaper price.

Bring a saucepan of water to the boil and carefully drop in
the corn cobs. Boil for 5–6 minutes until tender.

Heat the oil in a large frying pan over a medium–high heat
and cook the chilli flakes for 2 minutes to infuse the oil.

Use tongs to carefully place the par-cooked corn cobs into
the chilli oil. Sizzle for 4–5 minutes, turning frequently, and
allow the chilli-infused oil to coat all the corn.

Remove from the pan, then squeeze over the lime juice.
Generously sprinkle over the smoked sea salt and coriander,
just before serving.

carrot fries with cinnamon salt

These 'fries' are actually oven baked, making them a healthier, cheaper alternative to potato chips. You'll love the subtle hint of sweetness from the cinnamon.

Serves 2 generously

6 carrots, peeled and cut into 1 x 5cm (½ x 2in) batons

4 tbsp sunflower oil

½ tsp fine sea salt

Pinch of ground cinnamon

Preheat the oven as you're peeling and chopping the carrots into batons to ensure it's hot and ready to cook the fries in the fastest time.

Preheat the oven to 220°C/Gas mark 7.

Arrange the carrot batons in a single layer on two baking trays, then rub over the oil.

Bake for 13–14 minutes until softened.

In the meantime, mix together the sea salt and cinnamon.

Remove the carrot fries from the oven and scatter liberally with the cinnamon salt. Serve hot alongside the Fiery butternut squash ketchup (page 31).

parsnip fritters

When you have a couple of parsnips left over from making a roast dinner, grate them into these family-friendly fritters that little fingers will love.

Serves 4

6 tbsp sunflower oil

120g (4½oz) plain flour

1 tsp baking powder

1 tsp dried mixed herbs

Generous pinch of black pepper

½ tsp fine sea salt

2 medium parsnips, peeled and grated

I love serving these with a dip of cranberry sauce or Red mojo sauce (page 118).

Start heating the oil in a frying pan over a medium heat while you make the batter.

In a large bowl, mix together the flour, baking powder, mixed herbs, black pepper, and sea salt. Stir in the grated parsnip, ensuring it's coated in the flour mixture. Pour in 100ml (3½fl oz/scant ½ cup) of cold water and stir to form a batter.

Add tablespoon-sized portions of batter to the pan and cook for 2–3 minutes on each side until golden. Serve hot.

springtime pot au feu

Serve this vegan version of the classic French stew on a crisp, spring day, for a warming yet light alternative to a winter casserole. Ladle into deep bowls and pair with crusty bread for mopping. Asparagus is often considered a luxury item, however it is cost effective when eaten in season, during spring. Any leftovers can be frozen and enjoyed (on the cheap) when asparagus is out of season. If you can't source good value asparagus, simply add in a few more green beans.

Serves 2 generously

2 tbsp sunflower oil

1 medium leek, finely sliced

1 carrot, peeled and roughly sliced into rounds

1 stick of celery, roughly sliced

2 medium courgettes, chopped into 2cm (¾in) rounds

6 asparagus spears, sliced and tough stems discarded

8 green beans, trimmed and halved

2 cloves of garlic, peeled and crushed

1 tsp dried rosemary

1 tsp dried thyme

400g (14oz) can chopped tomatoes

800ml (scant 1½ pints/3½ cups) hot vegetable stock

Handful of frozen or fresh podded broad beans

Handful of flat-leaf parsley, finely chopped

Generous pinch of sea salt flakes and black pepper

Heat the oil in a large lidded saucepan over a high heat. Add the leek, carrot, celery, courgettes, asparagus, and green beans, cooking for 3 minutes until the vegetables begin to soften. Stir frequently to avoid sticking.

Add the garlic, rosemary, and thyme and cook for a further minute.

Pour in the chopped tomatoes, vegetable stock, and broad beans and loosely cover with the lid. Reduce the heat to medium and simmer for 10 minutes.

Remove from the heat, then scatter with the parsley, sea salt and black pepper. Serve hot.

To add a little heat to the dish, serve with a teaspoon of harissa per bowl. Harissa is a blend of chillies, spices, and tomatoes, traditionally used in North African dishes, but it lends itself well to lighter stews. You can buy harissa in supermarkets or Middle Eastern shops.

eastern cauliflower larb
with baby gem cups

Enjoy a meat-free, cost-effective twist on a traditional Thai classic. Pulsed cauliflower is combined with onion, lime juice, chilli, and fresh herbs. Load into leaves of baby gem lettuce for a light lunch or fresh dinner.

Serves 2 generously

---

1 large cauliflower, roughly cut into florets

1 tbsp sunflower oil

1 red onion, peeled and roughly sliced

2 cloves of garlic, peeled and finely sliced

1 red chilli, deseeded and sliced

2 tbsp light soy sauce

Juice of ½ unwaxed lime

2 spring onions, finely chopped

Generous handful of coriander, finely chopped

Generous handful of flat-leaf parsley, finely chopped

2 tbsp salted peanuts, roughly chopped

8 leaves of baby gem lettuce

Don't waste any of the cauliflower stem, it can all be used in the larb.

Put the cauliflower florets and stem in a food processor or blender and pulse until they resemble rice. Set aside.

Heat the oil in a large frying pan over a medium heat and cook the onion for 5 minutes until softened. Add the garlic and chilli and cook for a further minute.

Spoon in the pulsed cauliflower and soy sauce and stir through for 1–2 minutes to combine.

Remove from the heat and squeeze over the lime juice. Stir through the spring onions, coriander, parsley, and peanuts, then spoon into a large serving dish.

Serve the larb hot with cool baby gem lettuce leaves, spooning the larb into the lettuce cups just before eating.

mango gazpacho

During summer, look out for the abundance of mangos, with the best prices at fruit markets. If you think mangos are only for sweet recipes, try this fresh and fragrant three-step chilled gazpacho.

Serves 4

---

2 ripe mangos, peeled, chopped, and stone removed

300ml (½ pint/1¼ cups) pineapple juice, chilled

1 red pepper, deseeded and finely chopped

½ cucumber, finely chopped

2 spring onions, finely sliced

1 green chilli, deseeded and finely sliced

Generous handful of coriander leaves, roughly torn

Generous pinch of sea salt flakes

If you have the time available, chill the gazpacho for 2 hours before serving to allow the flavours to infuse further.

In a large bowl, blitz the mangos together with the pineapple juice using a hand blender, or add to a jug blender and blitz until completely smooth.

Stir through the red pepper, cucumber, spring onions, and chilli.

Scatter with the coriander and sea salt flakes just before serving.

cucumber salsa

Delicious served with Heritage tomato curry (page 97), or load into a baguette with hot, roasted vegetables.

Serves 4

½ cucumber, finely diced

2 spring onions, finely sliced

1 red chilli, deseeded and finely sliced

Zest and juice of ½ unwaxed lime

Handful of flat-leaf parsley, finely chopped

Drizzle of extra virgin olive oil

Pinch of sea salt flakes

Combine the cucumber, spring onions, chilli, and lime zest in a bowl.

Squeeze in the lime juice, then stir through the parsley. Allow to chill for 10 minutes.

Stir through the oil and sea salt flakes just before serving.

Revive a cucumber that looks past its best in this zingy salsa.

fig and tarragon stuffed pittas

Serve up a quick lunch by stuffing toasted pittas with tarragon-infused figs and lashings of vegan cream cheese. Delicious and decadent.

Serves 2

1 tsp sunflower oil

Pinch of dried tarragon

4 large fresh figs, sliced

2 white pitta breads

2 tbsp vegan cream cheese

Fresh figs require no special preparation; simply rinse and slice, removing just the tough top stem.

Rub a cold griddle pan with the oil, then sprinkle on the tarragon. Place the pan over a medium–high heat.

Use tongs to place the fig slices onto the griddle pan, then grill for 2–3 minutes on each side until soft and starting to caramelize.

Toast the pitta breads until crisp, then slit them to open the pocket. Carefully spoon in and spread the cream cheese.

Arrange the figs over the cream cheese and serve hot.

citrus fregola salad

This zesty, fresh, and fragrant salad makes the perfect garden lunch on a summer's day. Fregola is small, pea-shaped pasta, which cooks into soft little cushions. If you don't have fregola in the cupboard, giant couscous is an excellent substitute.

Serves 2

200g (7oz) fregola pasta
(ensure egg free)

1 orange, peeled and sliced into
rounds

1 grapefruit, peeled and sliced
into rounds

Zest of 1 unwaxed lime

2 generous handfuls of
watercress

Handful of basil leaves

Juice of 1 unwaxed lemon

Drizzle of extra virgin olive oil

Generous pinch of sea salt
flakes

Use the zest of an unwaxed
lime in this salad, then use the
lime juice to make Caribbean
sweet potato and coconut soup
(page 65).

Bring a saucepan of water to the boil and tip in the fregola. Simmer over a medium heat for 10 minutes until al dente.

In the meantime, add the orange and grapefruit slices to a bowl, then sprinkle over the lime zest. Mix in the watercress and basil, and leave to infuse.

Drain the water from the fregola and toss the fregola into the orange salad. Squeeze over the lemon juice and drizzle with the oil, then stir to combine.

Season with sea salt flakes and serve while the fregola is hot.

korean-style bibimbap bowls

Eat through the mountain of hot, sweet vegetables to a base of crisp, fried rice. Cooked, leftover basmati rice works best in this recipe, as it is fragrant and naturally starchy.

Serves 2

3 tbsp sunflower oil

6 tbsp cooked or leftover basmati rice

10 button mushrooms, brushed clean

4 radishes, finely sliced

1 carrot, peeled and very finely sliced

1 small courgette, very finely sliced

2 tbsp frozen or fresh podded edamame beans

Handful of spinach leaves

1 tbsp dark soy sauce

½ tsp soft brown sugar

1 red chilli, deseeded and finely sliced

1 spring onion, finely sliced

1 tbsp sesame seeds

There's no need to purchase pricey pre-cooked rice; simply simmer basmati rice for 12 minutes, drain, then allow to cool completely before using in this recipe.

Heat 2 tablespoons of the oil in a medium-sized frying pan over a medium–high heat, then add the cooked rice, pushing it down flat to form a level rice cake. Cook for 5 minutes until the base of the rice becomes crisp, then remove and separate into two bowls.

Heat the remaining tablespoon of oil in a large wok over a high heat and stir-fry the mushrooms, radishes, carrot, courgette, edamame beans, and spinach leaves for 2–3 minutes. Spoon in the soy sauce and brown sugar, then stir-fry for a further 2 minutes.

Spoon the vegetables over the rice, then scatter with the chilli, spring onion, and sesame seeds.

apple, borlotti, and chard cassoulet

Perfect as a main dish to your Sunday lunch, or as a midweek dinner served with crusty bread. If you have any left over, blend with vegetable stock for a smooth, flavourful soup.

Serves 4

---

1 tbsp sunflower oil

1 onion, peeled and finely chopped

2 carrots, peeled and sliced

1 stick of celery, diced

6 large leaves of chard, roughly sliced

1 tsp dried sage

½ tsp dried rosemary

Generous glug of red wine (ensure vegan)

4 eating apples, cored and sliced

400g (14oz) can chopped tomatoes

250ml (8¾fl oz/1 cup) hot vegetable stock

400g (14oz) can borlotti beans, drained and rinsed

Generous pinch of sea salt flakes

This cassoulet is a great way to use up apples, even if they are bruised or wrinkly.

Suitable for freezing.

Heat the oil in a large lidded saucepan over a medium heat and cook the onion, carrots, celery, and chard for 3 minutes until the onion begins to soften but not brown.

Sprinkle in the sage and rosemary, then pour in the wine and reduce down for 2 minutes. Add the apples and stir.

Pour in the chopped tomatoes and vegetable stock, then stir in the borlotti beans. Loosely cover with the lid and simmer for 10 minutes, stirring occasionally.

Season with sea salt flakes and serve hot.

heritage tomato curry

Summer is the season of great tomatoes, available in abundance, so their prices become affordable. But don't just stick to red salad tomatoes; mix it up with green, striped, vine, cherry, and golden! Look out at markets for a range of ripe tomato varieties, and also keep an eye on community allotment schemes where you can collect summer vegetables from a local grower for a small donation.

Serves 4

1 tbsp sunflower oil

1 onion, peeled and finely chopped

2 cloves of garlic, peeled and finely sliced

2cm (¾in) piece of ginger, peeled and grated

½ tsp dried chilli flakes

1 tsp ground cumin

1 tsp ground turmeric

1 tsp medium curry paste (ensure dairy free)

150ml (5¼fl oz/generous ½ cup) hot water

400g (14oz) can green lentils, drained and rinsed

500g (1lb 2oz) heritage tomatoes, small tomatoes halved; large tomatoes roughly quartered

Generous handful of coriander leaves

Juice of ½ unwaxed lemon

Generous pinch of sea salt flakes

Heat the oil in a large saucepan over a medium heat and cook the onion for 2 minutes until it begins to soften but not brown. Add the garlic, ginger, chilli flakes, cumin, and turmeric and cook for a further minute, stirring constantly.

Stir in the curry paste and pour in the hot water and lentils. Simmer for 8 minutes.

Add the halved and quartered tomatoes, stir to coat in the spiced lentil mix, and simmer for 3 minutes until the tomatoes are hot but keep their firmness.

Remove from the heat and stir through the coriander leaves and lemon juice. Season with sea salt flakes.

Have a jar of medium curry paste in the fridge, ready to pack in some concentrated flavour to any curry. Simply add a few extra store cupboard spices to the curry for a fragrant blend.

Suitable for freezing.

five-minute rainbow noodles

Cook up a rainbow in the kitchen with these 5-minute noodles. If you have time earlier in the day, finely chop the vegetables and keep them chilled before cooking them up for dinner.

Serves 2 generously

---

2 tbsp sunflower oil

¼ red cabbage, finely sliced

1 carrot, peeled and very finely sliced

1 yellow pepper, deseeded and very finely sliced

2 spring onions, roughly chopped

1 red chilli, deseeded and sliced

300g (10½oz) ready-to-wok soft noodles (ensure egg free)

2 tbsp sweet chilli sauce (ensure vegan)

Juice of ½ unwaxed lime

1 tbsp salted peanuts, roughly chopped

Handful of coriander leaves, roughly torn

Younger eaters will love these speedy and colourful noodles; simply omit the red chilli to reduce the heat.

Heat the oil in a wok over a high heat, then stir-fry the cabbage, carrot, yellow pepper, spring onions, and chilli for 2 minutes.

Add the noodles, then stir through the sweet chilli sauce and stir-fry for a further 2 minutes.

Squeeze in the lime juice and sprinkle with the peanuts. Scatter with the coriander leaves just before serving.

cajun-spiced potatoes

These spicy, fried potatoes make a tasty alternative to chips, or serve at breakfast with a few drops of Tabasco sauce for a fiery way to start the day! The potatoes cook best when they are in an even layer in the pan, so use two pans if you don't have one big enough.

Serves 4 as a side dish

2 large potatoes, cut into 1cm (½in) cubes

6 tbsp sunflower oil

1 yellow pepper, deseeded and finely sliced

1 tsp smoked paprika

1 tsp dried oregano

1 tsp mild chilli powder

½ tsp dried chilli flakes

Juice of ½ unwaxed lime

Generous pinch of smoked sea salt

There's no need to peel the potatoes as the skin adds extra flavour; just ensure that the potatoes are washed and scrubbed thoroughly.

Suitable for freezing.

Bring a large saucepan of water to the boil, then carefully add the potato cubes. Boil for 3 minutes, then drain on kitchen paper and dry all surfaces of the cubes.

Heat 5 tablespoons of the oil in a large frying pan over a medium–high heat, then carefully add the potatoes and yellow pepper. Cook for 5 minutes, turning the potatoes frequently.

Add the remaining tablespoon of oil, then sprinkle in the smoked paprika, oregano, chilli powder, and dried chilli flakes. Cook for a further 4 minutes, stirring frequently to avoid sticking.

Remove the pan from the heat and squeeze over the lime juice. Sprinkle with smoked sea salt and serve hot.

soy-roasted broccoli green curry

Broccoli takes on a wonderful, nutty flavour when roasted. Serve it over this Thai green curry for a simple dinner that is full of flavour. Frozen edamame beans are available in supermarkets or Chinese stores and last for ages in your freezer at home – simply take out the amount you need and cook from frozen.

Serves 2 generously

For the soy-roasted broccoli
220g (8oz) Tenderstem broccoli

1 tbsp sunflower oil

2 tbsp light soy sauce

1 tbsp sesame seeds

For the green curry
1 tbsp sunflower oil

2 cloves of garlic, peeled and crushed

4 spring onions, roughly chopped

2 tbsp frozen or fresh podded edamame beans

1 tbsp Thai green curry paste (ensure vegan)

400ml (14fl oz) can coconut milk

Generous handful of coriander leaves, roughly torn

1 red chilli, deseeded and finely chopped

Suitable for freezing.

Preheat the oven to 200°C/Gas mark 6.

Start by roasting the broccoli. Arrange the broccoli on a baking tray and drizzle with the oil. Use a pastry brush to liberally apply the soy sauce over the broccoli, then scatter with sesame seeds. Roast for 12 minutes until the broccoli has softened and the sesame seeds appear toasted.

In the meantime, prepare the green curry. Heat the oil in a large saucepan over a medium heat and cook the garlic, spring onions, and edamame beans for 2 minutes. Stir through the Thai green curry paste and pour in the coconut milk. Simmer for 10 minutes, stirring occasionally.

Remove the pan from the heat and stir through the coriander and chilli.

Remove the roasted broccoli from the oven and place over the green curry. Serve hot.

stir-fried beetroot, ginger and lemon

This may be your easiest stir-fry recipe yet! Pre-cooked beetroot is available in supermarkets for a great price, and tastes vibrant with chilli, ginger, lemon, and parsley. If you're using leftover rice, see the food safety tips on page 11. If not, simply cook some dried rice for 10 minutes while preparing the fresh ingredients. Pre-cooked pouch rice can be pricey, but it is convenient, so if you're in a rush, look out for special offers in supermarkets.

Serves 2 generously

---

1 tbsp sunflower oil

1 tsp dried chilli flakes

3cm (1¼in) piece of ginger, peeled and grated

1 clove of garlic, peeled and finely sliced

4 leaves of cavolo nero, stems discarded and roughly sliced

300g (10½oz) vacuum-packed cooked beetroot, drained and roughly sliced

200g (7oz) cooked or leftover rice

Juice of ½ unwaxed lemon

Handful of flat-leaf parsley, roughly chopped

Pinch of sea salt flakes

Sliced kale or savoy cabbage makes a great substitute for cavolo nero in this stir-fry.

Heat the oil in a wok over a high heat and cook the chilli flakes, ginger, and garlic for 1 minute to infuse the oil.

Throw in the cavolo nero and stir-fry for 2 minutes.

Add the beetroot and cooked rice. Stir-fry for a further minute, ensuring the beetroot keeps its firmness and shape.

Remove from the heat, squeeze over the lemon juice, and stir in the parsley. Season with sea salt flakes.

spicy satay skewers

Simple, grilled vegetables are served hot with a satay sauce that's made with store cupboard ingredients. Perfect for a spicy supper or to share at a barbecue.

Makes 4 skewers

For the vegetable skewers
12 button mushrooms, brushed clean

12 chunks of fresh or canned pineapple

1 red onion, peeled and quartered

4 baby corns, halved

1 green pepper, deseeded and cut into chunks

1 tbsp sunflower oil

For the satay sauce
1 tbsp sunflower oil

1 tsp dried chilli flakes

4 rounded tbsp smooth peanut butter

120ml (4fl oz/½ cup) hot water

1 tbsp dark soy sauce

2 spring onions, finely chopped

Serve these spicy skewers with Three-bean salad with mint and lime (page 107).

If you are using wooden skewers, soak them in water for about 10 minutes, or alternatively, use metal skewers.

Thread a button mushroom, a chunk of pineapple, a red onion quarter, a baby corn half, and a chunk of green pepper onto a skewer, then repeat until all the ingredients have been used.

Heat the oil in a griddle pan over a high heat. Place the skewers onto the hot griddle and cook for 3–4 minutes until slightly charred, turning with tongs frequently, then keep warm in a low oven.

To make the satay sauce, heat the oil and chilli flakes in a small saucepan over a medium–high heat for 1–2 minutes. Reduce the heat to low, then spoon in the peanut butter. Pour in the hot water and use a balloon whisk to beat until smooth. Stir through the soy sauce and spring onions.

Arrange the skewers on a serving plate, then pour over the satay sauce. Serve hot.

three-bean salad with mint and lime

Add this simple salad to your recipe collection for a delicious, filling, and healthy side dish or lunch.

Serves 4

400g (14oz) can cannellini beans, drained and rinsed

400g (14oz) can red kidney beans, drained and rinsed

400g (14oz) can borlotti beans, drained and rinsed

1 red onion, peeled and finely chopped

1 large tomato, finely chopped

Generous handful of mint leaves, finely chopped

Generous handful of flat-leaf parsley, finely chopped

Juice of 1 unwaxed lime

4 tbsp extra virgin olive oil

Generous pinch of sea salt flakes and black pepper

This salad will keep refrigerated in an airtight container for three days.

Mix together the cannellini, red kidney, and borlotti beans in a large bowl.

Stir through the red onion, tomato, mint, and parsley, then squeeze in the lime juice.

Refrigerate for 10 minutes, then drizzle with the olive oil and season with sea salt flakes and black pepper just before serving.

FAMILY FAVOURITES

breakfast rosti

I love serving these golden potato and spinach rosti for brunch, with herby mushrooms and tomatoes spooned over the top.

Serves 2

2 large baking potatoes, thoroughly washed

2 handfuls of spinach leaves

Pinch of nutmeg

Generous pinch of sea salt and black pepper

4 tbsp sunflower oil

8 closed-cup mushrooms, roughly sliced

5 cherry tomatoes, halved

½ tsp dried oregano

There is no need to peel the potatoes as the skins add extra flavour to the rosti.

Grate the potatoes onto a clean, dry tea towel, then squeeze out as much moisture as possible. Put the dry, grated potato into a bowl, then mix in the spinach leaves and nutmeg. Season with sea salt and black pepper.

Heat 3 tablespoons of the oil in a large frying pan over a high heat. Squeeze the grated potato together, shaping it into two dense masses. Carefully place into the hot frying pan and flatten with a spatula.

Fry for 5 minutes until golden, then flip and fry for 5 minutes on the other side.

In the meantime, heat the remaining tablespoon of oil in a separate frying pan over a medium heat and cook the mushrooms, cherry tomatoes, and oregano for 5–6 minutes until softened.

Carefully remove the rosti from the pan and place on serving plates. Spoon over the herby mushrooms and tomatoes. Serve hot.

chilli and ginger stir-fry sauce

Save money on shop bought stir-fry sauces by creating this five-ingredient sauce. Simply add your chosen vegetables to the wok after making the sauce, for a quick, budget-friendly meal. For added protein, throw in cashew nuts, peanuts, frozen edamame beans, or sesame seeds.

Serves 4

2 tbsp sunflower oil

1 tsp dried red chilli flakes

2cm (¾in) piece of ginger, peeled and grated

4 tbsp light soy sauce

Juice of 1 unwaxed lime

Heat the oil in a large wok over a high heat for 1 minute.

Add the chilli flakes and ginger and stir-fry for 2 minutes, then spoon in the soy sauce and cook for a further minute.

Squeeze over the lime juice after you've added the main bulk of the stir-fry (vegetables and vegan protein of your choice) to avoid any bitterness during cooking.

Store ginger root whole and peeled in the freezer and grate the amount you need from frozen to avoid waste and keep the flavour vibrant.

one-step pizza sauce

Homemade pizza is delicious, but don't waste money on pre-made pizza sauces. Throw in these store cupboard essentials for a herby, fresh purée to spread over your pizza base. Keep a few pitta breads in your freezer, ready to make delicious mini pizzas in less than 15 minutes.

Makes enough for 2 large pizzas

8 cherry tomatoes

½ tsp dried oregano

1 tbsp tomato ketchup

Generous drizzle of olive oil

Use a hand blender or jug blender to blitz the tomatoes, oregano, tomato ketchup, and oil to a smooth sauce. Liberally spread over pizza bases before adding your favourite toppings.

Olive oil gives a fruity, authentic flavour to the base, but sunflower oil also works well if that's what you have available. Suitable for freezing.

beetroot, lemon, and thyme orzo risotto

For a faster, cheaper way to cook risotto, switch the arborio rice for orzo pasta. It is shaped like grains of rice and doubles in size when cooked, but takes less than half the cooking time of risotto rice. This flavour combination is one of my favourites, with earthy beetroot, fresh lemon, and fragrant thyme.

Serves 2 generously

---

1 tbsp sunflower oil

1 onion, peeled and finely chopped

2 cloves of garlic, peeled and crushed

1 tsp dried thyme

250g (9oz) orzo pasta (ensure egg free)

500ml (17½fl oz/2 cups) hot vegetable stock

300g (10½oz) vacuum-packed cooked beetroot, roughly chopped

Juice of 1 unwaxed lemon

Generous pinch of sea salt and black pepper

You'll find vacuum-packed beetroot in supermarkets, saving you time pre-cooking the beetroot before use.

Heat the oil in a large saucepan over a medium heat and cook the onion and garlic for 2–3 minutes until softened but not browned, then add the thyme.

Pour in the orzo pasta and vegetable stock, then add the beetroot and any of its juice. Simmer for 10 minutes until the pasta has softened.

Remove from the heat and stir through the lemon juice. Season with sea salt and black pepper.

tea-infused chana masala

Allow chickpeas to be the star of the show in a fragrant, tea-infused sauce. Serve with warm naan breads and a spoonful of cooling vegan yoghurt.

Serves 4

---

1 tbsp sunflower oil

2 onions, peeled and finely diced

2 cloves of garlic, peeled and finely sliced

2 tsp garam masala

1 tsp ground turmeric

½ tsp dried chilli flakes

½ tsp cumin seeds

400g (14oz) can chopped tomatoes

2 x 400g (14oz) cans chickpeas, drained and rinsed

300ml (½ pint/1¼ cups) black tea

Generous pinch of sea salt flakes

Handful of coriander leaves, roughly torn

Juice of ½ unwaxed lemon

4 tbsp unsweetened soya yoghurt

Heat the oil in a saucepan over a medium–high heat and cook the onions for 2 minutes until they begin to soften. Add the garlic, garam masala, ground turmeric, chilli flakes, and cumin seeds, then cook for a further 2 minutes, stirring frequently.

Pour in the chopped tomatoes, chickpeas, and black tea, then cook for 10 minutes, stirring occasionally.

Remove from the heat and season with sea salt flakes. Scatter over the coriander leaves and squeeze over the lemon juice. Serve in bowls and spoon over 1 tablespoon of yoghurt on each. *+ pepper & onion sliced*

Allow the tea to infuse in boiling water while you are cooking the onions, garlic, and spices. Just remember to remove the loose leaves or tea bag before pouring the tea into the pan!

carrot, mango, and red onion ribbon salad

If you're looking for a colourful side to liven up a meal, simply throw together these ingredients and create a pretty, vibrant salad. Deliciously fresh with Tea-infused chana masala (page 115).

Serves 2

2 red onions, peeled and finely sliced

4 large carrots, peeled and shaved into ribbons using a vegetable peeler

1 mango, peeled, pitted and finely sliced

Generous handful of flat-leaf parsley, finely chopped

Juice of 1 unwaxed lime

Generous pinch of sea salt flakes

A good quality Y-shaped vegetable peeler works best to create the carrot ribbons. A great addition to your kitchen at a nominal cost.

Place the red onions in a heatproof bowl and pour over enough boiling water to cover. Allow to stand for 5 minutes to take away the acidity of the onions.

In the meantime, toss together the carrots and mango.

Drain away the water from the red onions, then rinse in cold water and pat dry. Toss the onions with the carrots and mango.

Stir through the parsley and lime juice. Season well with sea salt flakes.

aglio e olio

Simple and humble, this store cupboard spaghetti is an Italian family classic. The ingredients list may be underwhelming, but the finished dish is beautiful. It's worth using olive oil in this recipe, as it is the star of the dish. Avoid branded versions, and opt for own-brand varieties which will be significantly cheaper. It lasts well in the cupboard, and can be used in everyday cooking and roasting.

Serves 2

200g (7oz) dried spaghetti
(ensure egg free)

4 tbsp olive oil

3 cloves of garlic, peeled and
finely sliced

¼ tsp dried chilli flakes

Small handful of flat-leaf
parsley, finely chopped

Zest of ½ unwaxed lemon

Generous pinch of sea salt
flakes and black pepper

Throw in a handful of spring
greens or dark cabbage to the
spaghetti pan, if you have it
available and wish to add a
little extra to the dish.

Bring a large saucepan of salted water to the boil, then cook the spaghetti for 10 minutes until al dente.

In the meantime, heat the olive oil in a frying pan over a low–medium heat and cook the garlic and chilli flakes for 3 minutes until the garlic is just golden and has infused the oil.

Drain the spaghetti, then toss into the oil, stirring through to coat all the spaghetti in the fragranced oil.

Sprinkle over the parsley and lemon zest, then season with sea salt flakes and black pepper. Serve hot.

red mojo sauce

This fun and gently spiced sauce is a great way to encourage little (and big) kids to try new foods. Serve as a dip or drizzle over pasta or couscous, or stir through mashed potatoes. The sauce originates from the Canary Islands, where it is traditionally served with slow-roasted new potatoes.

Makes 1 small bowl

5 tbsp sunflower oil

2 red peppers, deseeded and roughly chopped

3 cloves of garlic, peeled and finely sliced

1 tsp sweet smoked paprika

1 tsp ground cumin

Pinch of dried chilli flakes

Handful of flat-leaf parsley leaves, roughly torn

Generous pinch of sea salt

Juice of 1 unwaxed lemon

Adjust the spice quantities to suit your taste.

Suitable for freezing.

Heat 1 tablespoon of the oil in a frying pan over a medium heat and cook the red peppers for 8 minutes until softened.

Add the garlic, paprika, cumin, and chilli flakes and cook for a further 2 minutes, stirring frequently to avoid burning.

Remove from the heat and spoon into a blender jug, or spoon into a large bowl if you are using a hand blender. Add the remaining 4 tablespoons of oil, the parsley, sea salt, and lemon juice. Blitz until completely smooth.

Spoon into a bowl and serve hot or cold.

chilli bean sliders

Treat yourself to these spicy, mini burgers. Little hands will love mashing and stirring the slider mix! Load with Sweetcorn salsa (page 61) and pickled gherkins.

Serves 4

2 x 400g (14oz) cans chilled kidney beans, drained and rinsed

1 yellow pepper, deseeded and finely diced

2 spring onions, finely chopped

Handful of coriander leaves, torn

4 tbsp rolled oats

1 tsp mild chilli powder

1 tsp smoked paprika

½ tsp fine sea salt

6 tbsp sunflower oil, for frying

8 mini white bread buns (ensure vegan)

4 pickled gherkins, sliced

Sweetcorn salsa (page 61), to serve

Keep the cans of kidney beans refrigerated before use, for a firmer mixture that is less likely to break in the pan.

Suitable for freezing.

In a large bowl, mash the chilled kidney beans using a fork (or squeeze in your hands) until just a few beans remain whole. The mixture should be semi-smooth.

Add the yellow pepper, spring onions, coriander, oats, chilli powder, smoked paprika, and sea salt, then stir until everything is combined into a dense mixture.

Heat the oil in a large frying pan over a medium heat. Make eight ball shapes from the bean mixture, then flatten into patties. Carefully place in the hot pan and cook for 4 minutes on each side, flipping with a spatula.

Serve the sliders in toasted or warmed mini bread buns, with sliced gherkins and a spoonful of sweetcorn salsa.

carrot and cardamom bisque

As much as I love a chunky, country-style soup, sometimes all you need is a smooth, rich bisque. Every indulgent spoonful has a silky mouthfeel, no one will ever know it's created in 15 minutes (and on a budget). Coconut milk is often cheaper in the world food aisle of supermarkets.

Serves 4

---

1 tbsp sunflower oil

1 onion, peeled and finely sliced

1 clove of garlic, peeled and finely sliced

4 large carrots, peeled and finely sliced

Seeds from 4 cardamom pods, ground

800ml (scant 1½ pints/3½ cups) hot vegetable stock

400ml (14fl oz) can coconut milk

Pinch of sea salt flakes and black pepper

Small handful of coriander leaves, to garnish

Slice the carrots very finely to ensure a fast cooking time.

Suitable for freezing.

Heat the oil in a large saucepan over a medium–high heat and cook the onion, garlic, carrots, and cardamom for 3 minutes, stirring constantly.

Pour in the vegetable stock and coconut milk, then bring to the boil and simmer for 10 minutes until the carrots have softened.

Pour the mixture into a jug blender or use a hand blender to blitz until completely smooth. Strain through a sieve to ensure it is completely smooth, then season with sea salt flakes and black pepper.

Ladle into warmed bowls and garnish with the coriander leaves just before serving.

lentil ragu

Rich ragu is always a crowd pleaser, with its moreish and satisfying flavour. This vegan version is ready in under 15 minutes! Serve over an egg-free pasta of your choice (I love it with tagliatelle).

Serves 4

1 tbsp sunflower oil

1 onion, peeled and finely diced

1 carrot, peeled and finely diced

1 stick of celery, finely diced

2 cloves of garlic, peeled and crushed

Generous glug of red wine (ensure vegan)

1 tsp dried mixed herbs

1 tsp dried oregano

400g (14oz) can chopped tomatoes

400g (14oz) can green lentils, drained and rinsed

6 cherry tomatoes, quartered

1 tbsp ketchup

Generous pinch of sea salt and black pepper

Handful of basil leaves, to garnish

Freeze into individual portions, then thoroughly reheat for a convenient weeknight meal.

Suitable for freezing.

Heat the oil in a large saucepan over a medium–high heat and cook the onion, carrot, and celery for 3 minutes until the vegetables begin to soften. Add the garlic and cook for a further minute.

Stir in the red wine, mixed herbs, and oregano and reduce for a further minute.

Pour in the chopped tomatoes, lentils, cherry tomatoes, and ketchup and cook for 10 minutes, stirring frequently.

Season with sea salt and black pepper, then scatter with the basil leaves just before serving.

giant spring rolls

I'm sure I don't speak for just myself when I say that I want more than a bite-sized spring roll. These large rolls are baked until they are crispy and golden, and are filled with hot, fragrant vegetables. Serve with a dip of Sweet chilli sauce (page 41).

Serves 4

1 tbsp sunflower oil

2 carrots, peeled and shaved into ribbons using a vegetable peeler

8 florets of Tenderstem broccoli, tough ends discarded

4 radishes, finely sliced

2 spring onions, roughly chopped

¼ savoy cabbage, finely sliced

1 tsp Chinese five-spice powder

1 tbsp light soy sauce

8 tortilla wraps

1 tsp sesame seeds

Sweet chilli sauce (page 41), to serve

Stir-fried radishes have a similar crunch to water chestnuts, but are much cheaper to buy.

Preheat the oven to 220°C/Gas mark 7.

Heat ½ tablespoon of the oil in a wok over a high heat and stir-fry the carrots, broccoli, radishes, spring onions, and cabbage for 1 minute. Spoon in the Chinese five spice and soy sauce and stir-fry for a further minute.

Place a tortilla wrap on a flat surface, then spoon in a ⅛ of the hot vegetable mixture on the right side of the wrap. Fold the bottom and top in towards the centre approximately 3cm (1¼in), then roll tightly from the right side to the left, rolling until it looks like a closed burrito. Repeat for the remaining giant spring rolls.

Place the rolls on a baking tray, then use a pastry brush to brush the remaining oil over the top and sides of the rolls. Sprinkle with the sesame seeds.

Bake for 10–12 minutes until the rolls are golden and crisp.

Serve with the sweet chilli sauce.

traditional greek fasolada

For an authentic taste of Greece, cook up this rustic soup, which is traditionally served with crusty white bread. It's a meal in itself when you're in need of something comforting, yet light.

Serves 4

2 tbsp olive oil

2 onions, peeled and finely chopped

2 carrots, peeled and diced

1 stick of celery, diced

1 tsp dried oregano

½ tsp dried thyme

½ tsp ground cinnamon

Pinch of sweet smoked paprika

400g (14oz) can chopped tomatoes

400g (14oz) can cannellini beans, drained and rinsed

800ml (scant 1½ pints/3½ cups) hot vegetable stock

Handful of flat-leaf parsley, roughly chopped

Generous pinch of smoked sea salt flakes and black pepper

Any white beans will work well in place of cannellini beans, including haricot butter beans.

Suitable for freezing.

Heat the oil in a large lidded saucepan over a medium–high heat and cook the onions, carrots, and celery for 3–4 minutes. Sprinkle in the oregano, thyme, cinnamon, and paprika and cook for a further minute.

Pour in the chopped tomatoes, cannellini beans, and stock and loosely cover with the lid. Simmer for 9 minutes, stirring occasionally.

Remove from the heat and scatter over the parsley. Season with smoked sea salt and black pepper and serve hot.

butter bean, lemon, and kale one-pot

This versatile dish makes for a hearty bowl of comfort food, or crush onto slices of toasted baguette for a simple crostini topping. Also delicious served cold as a sharing dish.

Serves 2 generously

---

2 tbsp olive oil

2 cloves of garlic, peeled and finely sliced

Pinch of dried chilli flakes

200g (7oz) kale, tough stems discarded and shredded

400g (14oz) can butter beans, drained and rinsed

Zest and juice of 1 unwaxed lemon

Handful of basil leaves

Generous pinch of sea salt flakes and black pepper

Remove the pan from the heat before stirring in the lemon zest and juice to stop the lemon flavour becoming bitter.

Heat the oil in a large frying pan over a medium heat and cook the garlic and chilli flakes for 2 minutes to infuse the oil.

Add the kale and butter beans and stir-fry for 5 minutes.

Remove from the heat and stir in the lemon zest and juice. Scatter over the basil leaves and season with sea salt flakes and black pepper.

serve ē hard boiled egg & bru

kedgeree with paprika yoghurt

Perfect for breakfast, brunch, lunch, or dinner, this kedgeree has plenty of dill and lemon and is great served hot with cooling salted yoghurt and paprika. A balanced dish that everyone will love.

Serves 2 generously

1 tbsp sunflower oil

1 onion, peeled and finely chopped

1 clove of garlic, peeled and crushed

1 tsp mild curry powder

½ tsp ground turmeric

½ tsp ground cumin

150g (5½oz) basmati rice

700ml (1¼ pints/3 cups) hot water

8 small florets of broccoli

8 green beans, halved

2 tbsp frozen peas

Handful of dill, finely chopped

Juice of ½ unwaxed lemon

2 tbsp unsweetened soya yoghurt

Pinch of fine sea salt

Sprinkle of smoked paprika

Heat the oil in a large saucepan over a medium–high heat and cook the onion and garlic for 2 minutes. Spoon in the curry powder, turmeric, and cumin and cook for a further minute.

Stir through the rice and pour in 500ml (17½fl oz/2 cups) of hot water. Simmer for 5 minutes, stirring frequently.

Add the broccoli and green beans and pour in the remaining 200ml (7fl oz/generous ¾ cup) of water, then cook for a further 4 minutes until the water has absorbed into the rice. Stir through the peas and cook for a further minute.

Remove from the heat and stir through the dill. Squeeze over the lemon juice and divide into two bowls.

Add 1 tablespoon of soya yoghurt over the kedgeree in each bowl and season with fine sea salt. Sprinkle a little sweet paprika over the yoghurt and serve.

I love adding green vegetables to the rice, including broccoli, green beans, and peas, but other quick-cook vegetables work well, including courgettes, spinach, and broad beans. Work with what you've got!

baked bean and sage pie

Homely flavours baked in a pie – and no one will know it was ready in 15 minutes. The trick is to cook the pastry topping separately to the beany filling, then simply place the pastry lid over just before serving. I love this cooked as one single pie (in a 20cm/8in pie dish), but it can be fun to have individual pies, served in ramekin dishes. Simply adjust the pastry to suit.

Serves 4

1 sheet of puff pastry (ensure dairy free)

1 tsp soya milk, for glazing

1 tbsp sunflower oil

1 onion, peeled and finely chopped

1 tsp dried sage

400g (14oz) can baked beans in tomato sauce

400g (14oz) can butter beans, drained and rinsed

1 tbsp tomato ketchup

Pinch of fine sea salt and black pepper

Many brands of shop-bought pastry are made using vegetable fats instead of dairy, making them "accidentally" suitable for vegans. Keep some in the freezer to make a quick family meal.

Suitable for freezing.

Preheat the oven to 200°C/Gas mark 6.

Lay out the puff pastry sheet and place your pie dish over it. Use a sharp knife to cut around the dish, then place the pastry oval/circle onto a baking tray. Brush the pastry with the soya milk, then bake for 10–12 minutes until golden and puffed.

In the meantime, make the pie filling. Heat the oil in a large saucepan over a medium heat and cook the onion and sage until the onion is translucent. Pour in the baked beans and their tomato sauce, the butter beans and tomato ketchup, and simmer on a low heat for 5 minutes, stirring frequently to avoid sticking.

Spoon the filling into the pie dish and season with sea salt and plenty of black pepper. Place the pastry lid over the filling and serve hot.

cupboard-raid sandwich spread

I always have a jar of this budget-friendly sandwich spread ready for creating tasty sandwiches. I love mine spread thickly, then loaded with rocket and olives. The beauty of this simple sandwich spread is that you can add the extras you have available, from a handful of flat-leaf parsley to sundried-tomatoes, or perhaps a drizzle of chilli oil.

Serves 4 generously

150g (5½oz) dried red lentils, rinsed

600ml (1 pint/2½ cups) hot vegetable stock

Drizzle of extra virgin olive oil

Juice of ¼ unwaxed lemon

Generous pinch of sea salt

Cooking the lentils in an 850W microwave is the key to the fast speed of this sandwich spread, but if you don't have a microwave, you can cook the lentils and stock in a pan for 25 minutes, over a medium heat.

Add the red lentils and 500ml (17½fl oz/2 cups) of the vegetable stock to a heatproof bowl and cook in a microwave for 14 minutes, stirring halfway through the cooking time.

Carefully remove from the microwave, then pour in the remaining 100ml (3½fl oz/scant ½ cup) of vegetable stock. Use a fork to gently mash down the lentils. Stir in the oil and lemon juice and season with sea salt.

Allow to cool, then keep refrigerated in an airtight jar for up to three days.

tortilla tacos with refried beans, carrot, chilli, and coriander

Crispy, golden tacos are filled with smooth refried beans, then topped with a bright carrot salsa. You'll never look at shop-bought tacos again! Serve with the Four-ingredient soured cream with chives (page 84).

Serves 4 (Makes 12)

For the tortilla tacos
3 tortilla wraps, cut into quarters

1 tsp sunflower oil

For the refried beans
1 tbsp sunflower oil

1 red pepper, deseeded and roughly chopped

3 spring onions, finely chopped

1 tsp mild chilli powder

1 tsp smoked paprika

1 tsp garlic powder

2 x 400g (14oz) cans pinto beans, drained and rinsed

Juice of ½ unwaxed lime

For the carrot salad
1 large carrot, peeled and grated

Generous handful of coriander leaves, roughly torn

1 small red chilli, deseeded and finely sliced

Generous pinch of smoked sea salt

Preheat the oven to 200°C/Gas mark 6.

Using two deep muffin trays, push a tortilla quarter into each mould to form a cup shape. Brush the edges with the oil, then bake for 8–10 minutes until crisp and light golden.

In the meantime, prepare the refried beans. Heat the oil in a saucepan over a medium heat and cook the red pepper and spring onions for 3 minutes until the pepper begins to soften. Spoon in the chilli powder, smoked paprika, and garlic powder and cook for a further minute. Tip in the pinto beans and stir to combine with all the spices. After 3 minutes, remove the pan from the heat, then mash the beans using a potato masher or fork until semi-smooth. Stir in the lime juice.

In a bowl, toss together the carrot, coriander, and chilli and season with smoked sea salt.

To assemble, remove the tortilla taco cups from the muffin pan and spoon in hot the refried beans, then load with the carrot, coriander, and chilli.

Pinto beans are traditionally used to make refried beans, and the canned variety mash down really well. If you don't have pinto beans available, red kidney beans make a good alternative, but will need a little more elbow-grease when mashing.

charred courgette and pesto tart

Create this simple yet delicious tart by baking the puff pastry in the oven while you grill the courgettes. This reduces the cooking time and prevents the dreaded 'soggy bottom'. Charred courgettes pair well with the flavour of fresh pesto, but experiment with other quick-cook green vegetables, including asparagus, broad beans, spinach, and peas.

Serves 4

1 sheet of puff pastry (ensure dairy free)

2 tsp unsweetened soya milk

1 tbsp sunflower oil

2 medium courgettes, sliced into rounds and ribbons

1 clove of garlic, peeled

Generous handful of basil leaves (reserve a few leaves for garnish)

1 tbsp flaked almonds

Juice of ¼ unwaxed lemon

Generous drizzle of extra virgin olive oil

Generous pinch of sea salt flakes and black pepper

Use up any remaining pesto as a flavourful topping for Carrot and cardamom bisque (page 122).

Preheat the oven to 220°C/Gas mark 7.

Place the puff pastry on a baking tray and fold over each of the four sides to create a 1cm (½in) border crust, then brush the border with the soya milk. Use a fork to lightly prick the inner section of the pastry. Bake for 10–12 minutes until the edges have risen and become golden.

While the pastry base is cooking, prepare the filling. Brush a griddle pan with the sunflower oil and place over a medium–high heat. Use tongs to lay the courgette rounds and ribbons onto the hot pan and cook for 5 minutes, then carefully turn and cook for a further 3 minutes.

To make the pesto, add the garlic, basil, and flaked almonds to a food processor or blender and blitz until semi-smooth. Pour in the lemon juice and extra virgin olive oil and blitz again to combine. Season with sea salt flakes. Alternatively, make the pesto by very finely chopping the garlic, basil, and flaked almonds before stirring in the lemon juice and extra virgin olive oil, then the seasoning.

Remove the pastry from the oven, then generously spread the inner section with some pesto. Arrange the courgettes neatly over the pesto, then brush the courgettes with a little more pesto. Scatter with a few basil leaves and season with black pepper.

herby hotpot

Serve this hotpot family-style, in a hob-to-table dish so everyone can tuck in!
Delicious with a side of lightly steamed broccoli. A winner with all the family.

Serves 4

For the crispy potato topping
4 tbsp sunflower oil

3 baking potatoes, thoroughly washed and finely sliced

For the hotpot
1 tbsp sunflower oil

1 onion, peeled and roughly chopped

1 medium leek, finely sliced

2 carrots, peeled and finely sliced

2 sticks of celery, roughly chopped

1 large parsnip, peeled and roughly diced

1 tsp dried mixed herbs

1 tsp dried rosemary

¼ tsp dried thyme

400g (14oz) can chopped tomatoes

200ml (7fl oz/generous ¾ cup) hot vegetable stock

1 tsp yeast extract

400g (14oz) can green lentils, drained and rinsed

Pinch of sea salt and black pepper

Start by making the crispy potato topping. Heat the oil in a large frying pan over a medium–high heat. Use tongs to carefully lay in the potato slices, then cook for 10–12 minutes, turning twice, until golden and beginning to crisp.

While the potatoes are cooking, work on the hotpot. Heat the oil in a lidded hob-to-table dish over a medium heat. Add the onion, leek, carrots, celery, and parsnip and cook for 3 minutes, stirring frequently. Add the mixed herbs, rosemary, and thyme and cook for a further minute.

Pour in the chopped tomatoes and vegetable stock, then stir through the yeast extract. Add the green lentils, then loosely cover with a lid and simmer for 10 minutes until the vegetables have softened.

Remove the dish from the heat and season with sea salt and black pepper. Arrange the crisp potatoes over the top and serve hot.

Cook the crispy potato topping separately to reduce the cooking time and have this hearty dish on the table in 15 minutes.

Suitable for freezing.

fuss-free burrito bowls

Load up your biggest serving bowls with fresh, zingy flavours using store-cupboard essentials and budget-friendly fresh ingredients. Who says you need to spend a fortune to create an Instagram-worthy burrito bowl?

Serves 4

200g (7oz) basmati rice

400g (14oz) can black beans, drained and rinsed

1 tsp Tabasco or hot sauce

Pinch of smoked sea salt

1 small red onion, peeled and finely diced

2 large tomatoes, roughly chopped

1 red chilli, deseeded and finely sliced

2 baby gem lettuces, finely shredded

1 red pepper, deseeded and finely sliced

200g (7oz) canned sweetcorn, drained and rinsed

Generous handful of coriander leaves, roughly chopped

Juice of ½ unwaxed lime

Add a spoonful of Two-minute BBQ mayonnaise (page 79) as a creamy, rich dip.

Start by cooking the basmati rice in a saucepan with cold water over a medium–high heat for 10–12 minutes until softened.

While the rice is cooking, combine the black beans, Tabasco, and smoked sea salt in a bowl. Divide into serving bowls.

In a separate bowl, mix together the onion, tomatoes, and chilli, then spoon this over the black beans.

Arrange a quarter of the lettuce and red pepper in each bowl.

Drain any remaining water from the rice, then stir in the sweetcorn and coriander. Squeeze over the lime juice and stir to combine. Spoon into the serving bowls and serve while the rice is hot.

SWEET TREATS

pear and chocolate crumble

Everybody loves a crumble. This economical pudding smothers sweet pears in a rich chocolate sauce, with a nutty, toasted topping. Canned pears are a great addition to your store cupboard as they don't need a long cooking time prior to enjoying. Serve with a scoop of dairy-free vanilla ice cream.

Serves 4

For the pear crumble

100g (3½oz) plain flour

50g (1¾oz) rolled oats

3 tbsp demerara sugar

2 tbsp vegan butter

1 tbsp of blanched hazelnuts, roughly chopped

200g (7oz) can pear halves, drained of juice

For the chocolate sauce

100g (3½oz) dark chocolate (ensure dairy free), broken into even pieces

150ml (5¼fl oz/generous ½ cup) sweetened soya milk

1 tbsp golden syrup

Cook the crumble topping separately to the pears to reduce the cooking time. It also keeps the topping crisper for the perfect crumble.

Preheat the oven to 200°C/Gas mark 6.

Start by preparing the pear crumble. In a mixing bowl, stir together the flour, oats, and sugar. Rub in the vegan butter until the mixture resembles breadcrumbs. Scatter in the hazelnuts, then spoon evenly onto a baking tray. Bake for 10–12 minutes until golden.

Arrange the pear halves into a heatproof dish and bake on the middle shelf of the oven for 10 minutes.

While the crumble topping and pears are cooking, make the chocolate sauce. Melt the chocolate in a saucepan over a low heat, stirring occasionally to distribute the heat and avoid burning. Use a hand whisk to whisk in the soya milk until combined. Remove from the heat and whisk in the golden syrup until the sauce appears rich and glossy.

Remove the pears and crumble topping from the oven. Divide the pears between your serving bowls and pour the chocolate sauce over them. Spoon over the crumble topping and serve hot.

cinnamon sugar tortillas

These sweet, crispy bites make for a delicious snack, especially for a big night in! I also love to serve them as wafers to vegan ice-cream sundaes. Vegan butter or margarine is readily available in supermarkets, with own brand versions being cheaper than the branded alternatives.

Serves 4

2 soft tortilla wraps, sliced in half, then cut into rough triangles

1 tbsp vegan butter

1 tsp granulated sugar

Pinch of ground cinnamon

These sweet tortillas will keep in an airtight container for up to three days.

Suitable for freezing.

Preheat the oven to 180°C/Gas mark 4.

Arrange the tortilla triangles on a baking tray, ensuring they don't overlap.

Melt the vegan butter in a saucepan or heatproof bowl in the microwave for 20–30 seconds, then use a pastry brush to lightly brush the butter over the tortilla triangles.

Sprinkle with half the sugar, then bake for 8–10 minutes until golden.

Remove from the oven, then sprinkle over the remaining sugar. Scatter with the cinnamon and serve warm or at room temperature.

cardamom kheer

Kheer is a popular Indian pudding, similar to rice pudding but with subtle spice from the cardamom and nutmeg. Traditionally, kheer uses basmati rice, but simple flaked pudding rice reduces the cooking time and is just as delicious.

Serves 4

150g (5½oz) flaked pudding rice

400ml (14fl oz) can coconut milk

2 tbsp granulated sugar

seeds from 3 cardamom pods, crushed

Pinch of ground nutmeg

Add the flaked pudding rice to a large saucepan, then pour in the coconut milk and 400ml (14fl oz/scant 1¾ cups) of cold water.

Stir in the sugar and cardamom seeds, then simmer for 10–12 minutes over a low–medium heat until thickened.

Remove from the heat and top with the nutmeg. Serve immediately.

Opt for full-fat coconut milk for a creamy texture in this pudding. The canned variety lasts for ages in the cupboard and is great to have on hand for a range of sweet and savoury recipes.

little lemon pots

If you're looking for a go-to dessert that you can whip up in mere moments, then this is the answer. Creamy and zesty pots, topped with a ginger biscuit crumb, are made using store cupboard and fridge essentials.

Serves 4

500g (1lb 2oz) plain soya yoghurt, chilled

1 tsp vanilla extract

Zest and juice of 1 unwaxed lemon

2 ginger biscuits (ensure vegan), crushed into fine crumbs

In a large bowl, use a hand whisk to combine the soya yoghurt, vanilla and lemon zest and juice. Whisk until silky and smooth.

Spoon into ramekins or small bowls, then sprinkle over the ginger biscuit crumbs just before serving.

Many brands of gingersnap-style biscuits are suitable for vegans, but do check the ingredients before buying.

toasted oat and roasted berry parfait

This refreshing yet substantial parfait is the perfect way to start your day. Toast the oats to enhance their flavour, then layer with cool vegan yoghurt and hot berries. Choose between frozen berries or seasonal fresh berries, or use a combination of both according to what you have available.

Serves 2

250g (9oz) frozen or fresh mixed berries

8 rounded tbsp rolled oats

Pinch of ground cinnamon

8 rounded tbsp plain soya yoghurt, chilled

Serve while the berries are warm to appreciate the delicious contrast between the roasted berries, cool yoghurt, and crunchy toasted oats.

Preheat the oven to 200°C/Gas mark 6.

Arrange the mixed berries on a baking tray, then roast for 10–12 minutes until softened.

In the meantime, add the oats to a frying pan and toast for 3–4 minutes over a medium heat until golden. Stir through the cinnamon, then remove from the heat.

Remove the roasted berries from the oven and spoon into tall glasses. Follow with the cool yoghurt and top with the toasted oats.

raspberry mojito jam

Shop-bought jam is cheap and simple, but can lack flavour. Pimp up your jar of raspberry jam with the flavours of a mojito, for a unique way to top your toast.

Makes 1 jar

300g (10½oz) shop-bought raspberry jam

10 fresh raspberries

8 mint leaves, finely chopped

Zest and juice of 1 unwaxed lime

Keep refrigerated for up to three weeks.

Spoon the raspberry jam into a saucepan and tip in the raspberries. Bring to a simmer over a low–medium heat for 2 minutes.

Add the mint and lime zest, them simmer for a further 2 minutes.

Remove from the heat and stir through the lime juice. Allow to cool slightly, then pour into a clean, dry jar and cool fully before refrigerating.

easter egg hot chocolate

Having excess chocolate around the house after Easter celebrations is never a bad thing, especially when you can whip up this decadent hot chocolate. Delicately spiced and lifted with freshly squeezed orange juice, treat yourself to a cosy drink that is so much better than any store-bought variety.

Serves 2

400ml (14fl oz/scant 1¾ cups) sweetened soya milk

100g (3½oz) dark chocolate (ensure dairy free), broken into even pieces

1 tsp light brown sugar

Juice of ½ unwaxed orange

Pinch of ground cinnamon

Pinch of ground nutmeg

Light brown sugar gives a caramel flavour to this drink, but it can be substituted with granulated white sugar for simple sweetness.

Heat the soya milk, chocolate, and sugar in a large saucepan over a low–medium heat for 4–5 minutes until the chocolate has melted, whisking throughout.

Whisk in the orange juice, cinnamon, and nutmeg until gently frothy.

Pour into mugs and serve hot.

three-ingredient banana pancakes

These fluffy pancakes are my favourite way to start the day. The riper the banana, the sweeter the pancakes, so use up that banana you're ready to throw away. Serve with toasted pecan nuts, vegan yoghurt and maple syrup if you happen to have some. Maple syrup can be expensive, however you can buy premium grade maple syrup from low-price supermarkets. It lasts for ages. If it is out of your price range, drizzle with golden syrup, or substitute for puréed seasonal soft fruits.

Makes about 9
small pancakes

---

1 tbsp sunflower oil, for frying

1 medium ripe banana, peeled

100g (3½oz) rolled oats

300ml (½ pint/1¼ cups) sweetened soya milk

These pancakes work well with any type of non-dairy milk you have available. For a nuttier flavour, try almond milk.

Heat the oil in a frying pan over a low–medium heat while you prepare the pancake batter.

Throw the banana, oats, and soya milk into a jug blender, or add the ingredients to a bowl and use a hand blender to blitz to a semi-smooth batter.

Add tablespoon-sized amounts of the batter to the hot pan, cook for 2 minutes until golden, then flip and cook the other side for a further 2 minutes. Serve hot.

sesame brittle thins

I love to snack on those little sesame snacks from the supermarket, but they don't come cheap. This two-ingredient recipe is simple, quick, and fuss-free.

Makes 1 tray

½ tsp sunflower oil, for greasing

5 tbsp sesame seeds

200g (7oz) caster sugar

These sweet thins will last for up to five days in an airtight container.

Rub the oil lightly onto a baking tray to prevent the brittle sticking.

Add the sesame seeds to a frying pan and toast over a low–medium heat for 2–3 minutes until golden, then transfer to a bowl and set aside.

Return the pan to the heat and sprinkle in the sugar. Leave for 5 minutes without stirring, until bubbling and light golden.

Stir in the toasted sesame seeds and remove from the heat.

Pour in a thin layer onto the prepared baking tray. Leave in a cool place for 5 minutes to set.

To break, cut into squares with a sharp knife, or make shards by dropping the baking tray onto a worktop.

peanut butter melt-in-the-middle chocolate pudding

Unexpected dinner guest? Mix up this decadent dessert in mere moments.

Serves 4 generously

For the peanut butter filling
3 rounded tbsp smooth peanut butter

100ml (3½fl oz/scant ½ cup) hot water

For the chocolate pudding
4 tbsp self-raising flour

2 tbsp cocoa powder

2 tbsp granulated sugar

2 tbsp sunflower oil

Serve with a generous scoop of vegan ice cream.

Start by making the peanut butter filling. Use a fork to whisk together the peanut butter and hot water until combined and smooth.

For the chocolate pudding, mix together the flour, cocoa powder, and sugar in a small, heatproof bowl. Spoon in the oil with 6 tablespoons of cold water and stir until combined.

Spoon out 1 rounded tablespoon of the cake mixture and pour the peanut butter filling into the resultant hole. Smooth over the removed cake mixture, covering any visible peanut butter.

Cook in an 850W microwave for 3 minutes, then allow to stand for 1 minute. Serve hot.

apple fritters

Sweet, hot, and a childhood favourite, these apple fritters are the perfect pudding or sweet snack for any time of the day.

Serves 2 generously

300ml (½ pint/1¼ cups) sunflower oil, for shallow-frying

200ml (7fl oz/generous ¾ cup) soya milk

2 tbsp soft brown sugar

1 tsp vanilla extract

120g (4oz) self-raising flour

¼ tsp ground cinnamon

2 large green apples, peeled, cored and finely sliced into rings

No apples? Pears also make delicious fritters.

Heat the oil in a large saucepan over a low–medium heat until hot.

In a large bowl, whisk together the soya milk, sugar, and vanilla until combined.

Sprinkle in the flour and cinnamon and whisk to a smooth batter.

Dip the apple rings into the batter, then use tongs or a slotted spoon to carefully drop them into the hot oil. Fry for 3–4 minutes until golden, then drain on kitchen paper. Serve hot.

peach melba smoothie

This smoothie makes a refreshing drink and is a great way to enjoy the convenience of canned peaches. If you don't have vanilla soya yoghurt available, plain soya or coconut also works well, but with a touch less sweetness.

Serves 2

400g (14oz) can peaches, drained and rinsed of syrup

2 handfuls of frozen or fresh raspberries, plus 4 for garnishing

200ml (7fl oz/generous ¾ cup) fresh orange juice

2 tbsp vanilla soya yoghurt

Add the peaches, raspberries, orange juice, and soya yoghurt to a jug blender, or use a hand blender, and blitz until completely smooth.

Pour into tall glasses and garnish with frozen or fresh raspberries.

Frozen raspberries make the smoothie ice cold, as well as being cheap and convenient to keep in the freezer.

coconut and cherry flapjack

Ideal for those times when you're in need of a homemade treat.

Makes 6 squares

4 tbsp golden syrup

4 tbsp sunflower oil

200g (7oz) rolled oats

50g (1¾oz) desiccated coconut

100g (3½oz) glacé cherries, halved

Mix up the flavour combination of this flapjack by substituting the glacé cherries for dried pineapple, cranberries, or papaya. Suitable for freezing.

Preheat the oven to 200°C/Gas mark 6.

In a large mixing bowl, whisk together the golden syrup and oil. Tip in the oats, coconut, and cherries, then stir to combine.

When all the oats are coated in the syrup mixture, press into a 12 x 8cm (6 x 3in) baking tray and bake for 10–12 minutes until golden.

Allow to cool, then cut into even squares.

coffee-poached figs with orange and hazelnuts

This is one of my favourite autumnal desserts, when figs are in season and at their best. After a hearty casserole or pie, a light pudding like this works a treat.

Serves 2

---

4 fresh figs, washed

500ml (17½fl oz/2 cups) strong black coffee

1 tbsp soft brown sugar

2 whole cardamom pods

Pinch of ground cinnamon

Zest of 1 unwaxed orange

Generous handful of blanched hazelnuts, roughly chopped

Serve with a spoonful of smooth vanilla soya yoghurt to contrast with the hot, poached figs.

Place the figs in a deep saucepan and pour in the coffee.

Spoon in the sugar, cardamom pods, cinnamon, and half of the orange zest, then simmer over a medium heat for 8–9 minutes until the figs are tender and the coffee sauce thickens slightly.

In the meantime, toast the hazelnuts in a frying pan for 2–3 minutes until gently golden.

Serve the poached figs in bowls, and ladle over a little of the coffee poaching sauce. Sprinkle over the toasted hazelnuts and remaining orange zest.

grilled pineapple, banana, and mango skewers with coconut and lime dip

Taste the tropics with these fruity grilled skewers! Fresh fruits work best here, as they will be firmer than their canned or frozen counterparts. Visit your local fruit market, where you'll likely pick up a bargain!

Serves 4

---

1 small pineapple, peeled and chopped into 5cm (2in) strips

1 mango, peeled, pitted and chopped into even chunks

2 bananas, peeled and thickly sliced

150ml (5¼fl oz/generous ½ cup) canned coconut cream, chilled

Zest and juice of 1 unwaxed lime

100ml (3½fl oz/scant ½ cup) orange juice, chilled

1 tbsp demerara sugar

Grill these fruit skewers on a barbecue for a summer treat that everyone will love.

If you are using wooden skewers, soak them in water for about 10 minutes; alternatively, use metal skewers.

Alternately thread the pineapple, mango, and banana onto the skewers.

Heat a griddle pan until hot, then place the fruit skewers onto the pan. Cook for 4–5 minutes, turning occasionally.

In the meantime, whisk together the coconut cream, lime zest and juice, and orange juice. Pour into a small bowl.

Carefully remove the griddle pan from the heat and sprinkle the fruit skewers with the sugar.

Serve hot with the cool dip.

index

acknowledgements

Writing my third book has been a pleasure, not only because I love showing people how to cook vegan food on a budget, but because I love working with the incredible people who make the book a reality.

Firstly, a huge thank you to all of the team at Quadrille. Special thanks to publishing director Sarah Lavelle, for believing in this book, and believing in me. Heartfelt thank you to commissioning editor Zena Alkayat for making this book a reality, and excellent attention to detail throughout. Further thanks for the editorial support to Corinne Masciocchi.

Thank you to the talented Claire Rochford and Katherine Keeble from the design team for the beautiful vision and layout of the book. Words can't describe how thankful I am to senior publicist Rebecca Smedley – I love working with you, and your emails always bring a smile to my face!

To my creative A-Team. Thank you to photographer Dan Jones and assistant Aloha Bonser Shaw for the wonderful photographs; it is always fantastic to work with you. To the fabulous food stylist Emily Ezekiel, and talented assistant Kitty Coles, you are wonderful, and I am eternally grateful for your skills, creativity (and girly gossips) during the shoot. I look forward to working with you all again.

This wouldn't be possible without my wonderful literary agent Victoria Hobbs at A.M. Health – you are a legend! Thank you for your guidance and advice, always.

Ever loving thank you to my wonderful Mum and Dad, whose advice is to follow your dreams, no matter what. I am so lucky to have you as parents! Thank you to my gorgeous sister Carolyne, and brilliant brother-in-law Mark for your encouragement and support. To my most important critics – my nieces Tamzin and Tara. It is wonderful to see you growing up with a love of cooking and food, a care for animals and the world around you. Thank you also to Auntie May for your love and support – it does not go unnoticed.

To my inspirational best friends Mary-Anne, Louise, Charlotte, Amelia, Emma, Amy and Katie. Thank you for all of the laughs, texts, coffees and friendship.

Thank you to Dudley, my favourite fluffy writing partner, you are a dream.

To my wonderful fiancé David, thank you for your love and support, through the good times and the hard times. What an exciting time we have to look forward to!

publishing director: Sarah Lavelle

editor: Zena Alkayat

designer: Katherine Keeble

photographer: Dan Jones

photographer's assistant: Aloha Bonser Shaw

food and props stylist: Emily Ezekiel

assistant food stylist: Kitty Coles

production: Tom Moore, Vincent Smith

First published in 2019 by Quadrille, an imprint of Hardie Grant Publishing

Quadrille
52–54 Southwark Street
London SE1 1UN
quadrille.com

Cataloguing in Publication Data: a catalogue record for this book is available from the British Library.

Text © 2019 Katy Beskow
Photography © 2019 Dan Jones
Design and layout © 2019 Quadrille Publishing

ISBN: 978 1 78713 255 9

Printed in China